Teaching Composition
as a Social Process

Teaching Composition as a Social Process

BRUCE McCOMISKEY

UTAH STATE UNIVERSITY PRESS
Logan, Utah

Utah State University Press
Logan, Utah 84322-7800

Portions of this book were published originally as the following:
"Composing Postmodern Subjectivities in the Aporia between Identity and Difference."
   Rhetoric Review 15: 350-64. Copyright 1997 by *Rhetoric Review*; reprinted by permission of *Rhetoric Review*.
"Postmodern Cultural Studies and the Politics of Writing Instruction." *TETYC* 26:
   144-53. Copyright 1998 by the National Council of Teachers of English. Reprinted
   with permission.
"The Post-Process Movement in Composition Studies." In *Reforming College Composition*,
   ed. Wallace, Jackson, and Lewis. Copyright 1999 by Greenwood/Heinemann, an
   imprint of Greenwood Publishing Group, Inc., Westport, CT.
"Social-Process Rhetorical Inquiry: Cultural Studies Methodologies for Critical Writing
   about Advertisements." *JAC* 17 (1997): 381-400.
"Writing in Context: Postmodern Theory and Practice in the Composition Class."
   Composition Forum 8 (1997): 32-41.

This book was typeset, printed, and bound in the United States of America.
Typography by WolfPack.
Cover by Stephen Adams.

Library of Congress Cataloging-in-Publication Data

McComiskey, Bruce
Teaching composition as a social process / Bruce McComiskey. p. cm.
ISBN 0-87421-283-9
1. English language—Rhetoric—Study and teaching—Social aspects. I. Title.
PE1404 .M387 2000
808'.042'07—dc21
99-6774
CIP

for Cynthia and Celia

CONTENTS

ACKNOWLEDGMENTS

MANY STUDENTS, TEACHERS, FRIENDS, AND COLLEAGUES HAVE CONtributed greatly to this project. Writing is, of course, a social process, and I could never have composed this manuscript without their engaging conversations and critical readings. I would first like to thank my colleagues and friends who read portions of this book while it was still in draft form, including Cynthia Ryan, John Trimbur, Todd Goodson, Frank Farmer, Jeffrey Williams, and Tracey Baker. I would also like to thank Utah State University Press director, Michael Spooner, and USUP's anonymous reviewers for their encouragement and helpful comments. Many thanks are also due to those who, over the past two decades and in various ways, have encouraged my love for writing and teaching, especially Jan Neuleib, Edward Schiappa, Janice Lauer, James Berlin, and my father Thomas McComiskey.

Of course, any project like this would simply be incomplete without a heartfelt thank-you to all the students who took the courses and responded to the assignments described here. Even the most soundly designed curriculum cannot succeed without dedicated students to engage it.

Parts or all of some chapters in this book have appeared elsewhere. Thanks to the publishers of *Composition Forum*, *JAC*, *Rhetoric Review*, *TETYC*, and of the book *Reforming College Composition* for their generous permission to reprint. Full citations appear on the copyright page.

INTRODUCTION

MY CAREER AS A WRITING TEACHER BEGAN IN THE EARLY 1980S, when I was an undergraduate teaching assistant in the composition program at Illinois State University, and since that time I have been a card carrying . . . well, everything. At first, I was intoxicated by the expressivist fervor for individuality and creativity, reading Donald Murray and Peter Elbow on busses home from college and, later, grad school. Yet at times I was uncomfortable in the classroom, lacking concrete strategies to help my students solve important rhetorical problems. Soon after this, and partly the result of a "quest" for something more, I began to read the Carnegie Mellon cognitivists, Linda Flower and John Hayes, and I found that certain aspects of the writing process could in fact be identified and taught. But their cognitive process model began to look too much like a computer model, with input, output, and (micro)processing in the middle. So I still felt uncomfortable in the classroom. During my graduate studies at Purdue University in the late 1980s and early 1990s, though, I encountered James Berlin.

You might think the story continues like this: ". . . and I discovered the error of my ways." But it doesn't continue that way, or at least not that simply. Jim Berlin had a tremendous impact on my career. I found new energy in the social theories we applied to composition in his graduate classes, yet I missed the pragmatic power I used to feel from teaching the writing process. A lot of the essays we read then, ones that elaborated social theories of composition, and many that I study now, use what I call the *read-this-essay-and-do-what-the-author-did* method of writing instruction: read Roland Barthes's essay

"Toys" and write a similar essay on a toy of your own choice; read John Fiske's essay on TV and critique a show.

Although I am obviously a strong advocate of social approaches to teaching writing, I oppose composition courses that draw on cultural theory as content and revert unnecessarily to product-centered pedagogical practices. These "social-content" composition courses foreground cultural politics as material to be mastered, and students write to demonstrate what they have learned. In these classes, teachers and assigned texts pre-judge the ethical character of the social institutions and cultural artifacts under study even before students have had the chance to critique the institutions and artifacts for themselves; and because predetermined ethical judgments are the content of these courses, students are not encouraged to view writing as an epistemic process.

Yet even as early as 1987, Karen Burke LeFevre urged us to view invention as a social act. The strategies I had come to associate with expressivist and cognitivist pedagogies, LeFevre argued, were not rightly their sole province. I began, then, from the early 1990s onward, to explore what "social-*process*" writing instruction might look like.

What I believe "social-content" composition courses miss is the fact that critical theorists, like Barthes, Fiske, and many others, develop over the years complex heuristics through which they approach their subjects; the finished text of Barthes's *Mythologies*, for example, actually masks the heuristic process that Barthes undertook to compose the published version of his famous book. Barthes, in other words, had developed a complex set of *topoi* that he could use to direct his attention here and there in the composing process, and these *topoi* are simply not able to be deduced only from reading his essay on toys (or even from reading the entire collection). This problem of the "mythologized" process leaves students in "social-content" composition classes with an impossible task—write an essay like Barthes's, but do it without the kind of heuristic processes from which he was able to draw.

Let me provide a more concrete example of the kind of heuristic I am describing. Since Karl Marx's "Introduction to the Critique of Political Economy" was published, many leftist and Marxist social theorists have used the cycle of production, distribution, exchange, and consumption, which Marx describes there in detail, as a guide for cultural critique. And within each of these "moments" in the cycle, critics ask questions of themselves and the objects of their analysis—not questions that unleash the creative linguistic potential of socially unsoiled individuals, not questions that harness the power of the mind's cognitive structure, but questions that direct a writer's attention toward subjects and strategies that lead to productive critical writing.

Social-process composition pedagogies treat critical writing as rhetorical inquiry and political intervention into the cultural forces that construct our subjectivities. Composing processes remain the focus of these pedagogies, but composing is always situated within particular socio-political contexts rather than within autonomous individuals or structured minds. Recent attempts to contextualize the writing process have focused on ways in which cultural forces, such as social narratives and ideologies, influence the act of composing. In "Rhetoric and Ideology in the Writing Class," for example, James Berlin describes the writing process as a dialectical interaction among material conditions, social ideologies, and individual interpretations, all inevitably imbricated within historically specific economic, social, and political contexts (488-93). Assigned texts in social-process composition courses represent diverse ideological perspectives against which students construct their own critical perspectives on social institutions and cultural artifacts—these texts are not content to be learned but positions to be negotiated. Yet, as I have indicated, assigned readings are neither the only nor the best social-process heuristics available to writers and teachers; social theory offers a wealth of critical methodologies for interrogating social institutions and cultural artifacts, and these methodologies easily convert into rhetorical heuristics that guide writing processes in a variety of economic, cultural, political, and social contexts.

Teaching Composition as a Social Process is my response to some of the concerns I have raised in this brief introduction, as well as many more concerns that will be raised throughout the remaining pages. Chapter one attempts in a modest way to re-map composition studies and place "social-process" pedagogies within a larger scheme of textual, rhetorical, and discursive concerns. In chapter two, the focus turns more explicitly to what I have called "social-process rhetorical inquiry," a collection of cultural studies methodologies based on the cycle of cultural production, contextual distribution, and critical consumption, and chapter three locates this social-process pedagogy within the "post-process" movement in composition studies. Chapter four extends the focus of chapter three, exploring the nature of postmodern subjectivities and their impact on "post-process" composing in the contexts of rap music and work.

The final two chapters of *Teaching Composition as a Social Process* explore social-process/post-process composition studies with "schooling" as their central theme. In chapter five, I turn to critical discourse analysis (a complex theoretical and methodological integration of linguistics, rhetoric, and discourse studies) as a framework for writing assignments focusing on the critique and production of college viewbooks, and chapter six examines the impact of postmodern culture on students' "academic" identities.

Each chapter in this book describes aspects of social theories that I believe have important relevance for composition studies, and most chapters also present and illustrate heuristics for rhetorical inquiry based largely on these social theories. These heuristics are intended to guide student inquiry and instructional practice, not to restrict them. In other words, unlike highly structured heuristics such as the tagmemic grid, the heuristics described here are intended to be negotiated: students should use the heuristics in ways that suit them most, and teachers should present aspects of the heuristics that serve their own pedagogical goals.

Much of the social theory discussed throughout this book adopts a postmodern stance (to widely varying degrees), and from a postmodern perspective, heuristic inquiry does not serve the creative needs of autonomous individuals or the cognitive needs of structured minds. Instead, postmodern heuristic inquiry provides options for rhetorical exploration within social contexts, and, most importantly, as these contexts change, so too must the heuristics we use to guide us and our students through the critical writing process.

CHAPTER ONE

Three Levels of Composing

OVER THE YEARS, SOME SCHOLARS IN RHETORIC AND COMPOSITION have proposed frameworks attempting to "map" composition studies, plumb the depths of its scope, define the borders that divide its practitioners into camps. Richard Fulkerson's four philosophies of composition (mimetic, expressive, formalist, and rhetorical) and James Berlin's major pedagogical theories (current-traditional, expressivist, cognitivist, and epistemic) have served, and serve now, as foundations, schemes, terministic screens through which to structure composition studies as a disciplinary formation. But one characteristic of these maps of composing, a characteristic I have found less and less helpful, especially in recent years, is their attempt to divide writing teachers into separate and unequal categories. While Fulkerson says that all four philosophies have value, he clearly prefers the rhetorical approach, and—without hedging—Berlin tells us that he favors epistemic rhetoric.

At East Carolina University, where I was an Assistant Professor of rhetoric and composition from 1994 to 1998, I taught several sections of "Teaching Composition: Theory and Practice," a graduate-level seminar designed to introduce teaching assistants (trained mainly in literary studies) to the major concepts and methodologies involved in the teaching of writing. I always began these courses with a discussion of Fulkerson's philosophies and Berlin's theories as a way of providing my students with schematic reference points, categories into which they could place the articles and textbooks we would examine throughout the semester. What I found, however, was that these students resisted Fulkerson and Berlin. They did not want to "camp out"; they wanted to "forage." These students hyphenated themselves: "I'm a rhetorical-expressivist" or "I'm an epistemic-formalist."

At first I was concerned, a bit unsettled, but then I remembered Berlin's caution regarding his own scheme for composition studies. In the "Postscript" to *Rhetoric and Reality*, Berlin confesses

> the taxonomy I have used in discussing rhetoric and writing up to 1975 does not prove as descriptive after this date. The most important reason for this has been the tendency of certain rhetorics within the subjective and transactional categories to move in the direction of the epistemic, regarding rhetoric as principally a method of discovering and even creating knowledge, frequently within socially defined discourse communities. (183)

Fulkerson and Berlin's maps of composition studies, then, represent the discipline as it has been (i.e., there is historical validity to their maps), but I believe that they do not represent the discipline as it is now or will be in the new millennium. Some important recent work, such as Linda Flower's *The Construction of Negotiated Meaning* and Sherrie Gradin's *Romancing Rhetorics,* for example, constructs compound nouns that two decades ago would have been considered oxymorons: Flower calls her study a "social cognitive" theory of writing, and Gradin refers to her work as "social expressivist." Integration and negotiation are defining the future of composition studies, not division and categorization.

In this chapter, I offer a new map of composition studies, a map that does not focus on the borders that separate us as writing teachers; instead, it is a map that illuminates our commonalities. This new map of composition studies represents three levels of composing: textual, rhetorical, and discursive. At the textual level of composing, we focus our attention on the linguistic characteristics of writing. At the rhetorical level, we focus on the generative and restrictive exigencies (audience, purpose, etc.) of communicative situations. And at the discursive level of composing, we focus our attention on the institutional (economic, political, social, and cultural) forces that condition our

very identities as writers. This tripartite map of composing illuminates our commonalities as writing teachers because all of us instruct
students at all three levels, whether we do it consciously or not.

While historically writing teachers have overtly focused their
pedagogical energies at the textual and rhetorical levels, the discursive level of composing has received a great deal of attention in
recent years. This attention to writing at the discursive level has met
some opposition, of which Maxine Hairston's "Diversity, Ideology,
and Teaching Writing" is representative. Yet we learn from many
who have responded to Hairston that even her own composition
pedagogy is steeped in "individualist" ideological strategies, and the
greatest danger of all is leaving those strategies unexamined.[1]

I argue that a balanced approach to the three levels of composing
leads students to the fullest and most effective understanding of their
writing processes. To this end, I believe that we need to make all
three levels *overt* in our composition classes, perhaps even guiding
students through peer review cycles and formative teacher comments
that attend to each of the three levels of composing.

I begin this chapter by illustrating the textual, rhetorical, and discursive levels of composing with specific reference to the concept of
audience; I begin with audience because of its mutability, changing its
very nature with the constraints of each new turn in composition theory and practice. (It is not my goal to represent audience theory in its
entirety; I refer, instead, only to some of the best-known sources over
the past few decades as examples of the transformations "audience"
has undergone.) Next, I discuss a heuristic for analyzing the "audience
awareness" of documents, especially student papers, at the textual,
rhetorical, and discursive levels, and I apply this heuristic to a letter
that one student wrote about the condition of the bathrooms in his
dormitory. Finally, I address the need for an integrated writing pedagogy that maintains attention to all three levels of composing.

AUDIENCE AND THE LEVELS OF COMPOSING

Audience manifests itself at the textual level of composing as a
"fiction" or as "audience invoked." In "The Writer's Audience Is

Always a Fiction," for example, Walter Ong argues that rhetorical conceptions of audience in times of orality were dominated by the immediate presence of listeners, causing orators to view audiences as external to speech. But with the emergence of new communication technologies and the prominence of text-literacy in modern cultures, real audiences disappear from view and reassert themselves as linguistic characteristics of the very texts we read and write. Ong explains, "If the writer succeeds in writing, it is generally because he can fictionalize in his imagination an audience he has learned to know not from daily life but from earlier writers who were fictionalizing in their imagination audiences they had learned to know in still earlier writers, and so on back to the dawn of written narrative" (11). The skill of adapting written texts to particular audiences, then, is not learned through verbal interactions but through the interactions of readers and writers mediated by texts. Thus, Ong continues, all writers "fictionalize their audiences, casting them in a made-up role and calling on them to play the role assigned" (17). Writers inject these "made-up roles" into texts through linguistic cues that guide audiences through the reading process. For example, Ong argues that Ernest Hemingway in *A Farewell to Arms* fictionalizes his audience, guides his audience into a "familiar" or "you-and-me" role through his specific use of "the definite article as a special kind of qualifier" and "the demonstrative pronoun 'that'" (13).

While Ong believes that audiences are only "present" in oral communication and "fictionalized" in written communication, Douglas Park, Russell Long, Lisa Ede, and Andrea Lunsford contend that audiences affect the writing process both as a quality of texts themselves and as a complex web of rhetorical constraints that condition the production of texts. As Park suggests, the "meanings of 'audience,' then, tend to diverge in two general directions: one toward actual people external to a text, the audience whom the writer must accommodate; the other toward the text itself and the audience implied there, a set of suggested or evoked attitudes, interests, reactions, conditions of knowledge which may or may not fit with the qualities of actual readers or listeners" (249). Both Park and Long concur that these latter textual audiences—the "features of the text" that signify an awareness of audience (Park 250), the "signals provided by the writer for his audience" (Long 225)—are the most important manifestations of audience for teachers and students to consider in the writing process.

Audience manifests itself at the rhetorical level of composing as "audience addressed." Ede and Lunsford agree with Park and Long that "Those who envision audience as invoked stress that the audience of a written discourse is a construct of the writer" (Ede and Lunsford 160). But while Long and Park suggest that text-based conceptions of audience are the most crucial ones to which writers must attend, Ede and Lunsford, on the other hand, argue for a more integrated, rhetorical approach to audience. An addressed audience is one that is "present" to the rhetorical situation. According to Ede and Lunsford, "Those who envision audience as addressed emphasize the concrete reality of the writer's audience; they also share the assumption that a knowledge of this audience's attitudes, beliefs, and expectations is not only possible (via observation and analysis) but essential" (156). Yet Ede and Lunsford argue that the "most complete understanding of audience thus involves a synthesis of the perspectives" called audience addressed and audience invoked. The term "audience," Ede and Lunsford suggest, "refers not just to the intended, actual, or eventual readers of a discourse, but to all those [whether invoked or addressed] whose image, ideas, or actions influence a writer during the process of composition" (168).

At the discursive level of composing, we move from the writer's conscious choices to the social composition of the writer and the institutional contexts in which composing takes place. In *Audience and Rhetoric*, James Porter argues that students must understand writing at the discursive level in order to compose effective documents of their own (105-17), and in *Rhetorics, Poetics, and Cultures*, James Berlin similarly contends that "the more the writer understands the entire semiotic [or discursive] context in which he or she functions, the greater the likelihood that the text will serve as an effective intervention in an ongoing discussion" (130). Without a solid understanding of a text's context, of a community's "rules" for communication as a whole, a writer's message, however elegant or rational, may never be taken seriously.[2] From a discursive perspective, culture and writing are inseparable—there is no writing without culture, and there is no culture without writing. Richard Harvey Brown highlights this social-discursive interaction, suggesting that "social structures can be understood as structures of language and these structures are invented through acts of speech" (227). Further, according to cultural studies historian Graeme Turner, discourse "refers to socially produced groups of ideas or ways of thinking that can be tracked in individual texts or groups of texts, but that also demand to be located within wider historical and social structures or relations" (32-33).

Audience manifests itself at this discursive level of composing as "community" and "culture." Toward the end of "Audience Addressed/Audience Invoked," Ede and Lunsford illustrate their integrated, rhetorical approach to audience by discussing the complex audience concerns (both addressed and invoked) they had as they collaboratively composed the essay, and they conclude with the following observation: "And after the essay is published, we may revise our understanding of audiences we thought we knew or recognize the existence of an entirely new audience" (168). This is, I believe, what has happened, and Lunsford and Ede explore this possibility of a new conception of audience—a *discursive* conception—in "Representing Audience." Here Lunsford and Ede attempt a self-critique of their earlier essay, "Audience Addressed/Audience Invoked," and they subject this "earlier work to critical inquiry in an effort to foreground the rhetoricity of this work and to explore and learn from the cultural, disciplinary, and institutional forces at play in it" (169). Lunsford and Ede, for example, no doubt influenced by the recent "social turn" (Trimbur) in composition studies, recognize that their earlier essay neglected crucial discursive pressures on composing:

> Although we recognize in AA/AI that students have less power than teachers and thus less freedom in some rhetorical situations than in others, we do not pursue the multiple ways in which the student writer's agency and identity may be shaped and constrained not only by immediate audiences but also, and even more forcefully, by the way in

which she and those audiences are positioned within larger institutional and discursive frameworks. Nor do we consider the powerful effects of ideology working through genres, such as those inscribed in academic essayist literacy, to call forth and thus to control and constrain writers and audiences. (170-71)

And, Lunsford and Ede continue, "Teachers and students are—we understand now better than in the past—not free individual agents writing their own destinies but rather constructed subjects embedded in multiple discourses, and the classroom is not a magic circle free of ideological and institutional influence" (173). Identities, ideologies, frameworks—these are the constraints placed on both writers and audiences at the discursive level of composing processes.

TOWARD AN INTEGRATED THEORY OF COMPOSING

I argue that careful attention to all three levels of composing (in relation to every aspect of writing and its situations, not just audience) characterizes successful writing processes. In other words, excessive attention to just one level, whether textual, rhetorical, or discursive, gives students a limited, unbalanced, and, I believe, inaccurate view of how writing works. Writing courses that focus too much on the textual level of composing tend to be courses in grammar and style, neglecting the pressures placed on writing by specific rhetorical situations. Courses focusing too much on the rhetorical level tend to highlight revision and audience ("addressed") awareness, neglecting the impact existing texts and social institutions have on students' writing processes. And courses that focus too much on the discursive level tend to be courses in cultural studies, neglecting the writing process altogether. To illustrate the interconnectedness of the three levels of composing and the importance of balance among them, I will first present a heuristic for analyzing the audiences of documents at the textual, rhetorical, and discursive levels, and then I will apply this heuristic to a student's letter on the condition of the men's bathroom in his dorm. (The heuristic is by no means complete, nor is it intended to be; different teachers will, of course, develop different questions representing their own pedagogical concerns.)

Heuristic: Analyzing Audiences

Textual Level

Format: How does the format of the text call the audience into a specific role?

Style: How does the style of the text call the audience into a specific role?

Genre: How does the genre of the text call the audience into a specific role?

Rhetorical Level

Writer's Role: How does the writer define her role in relation to the audience?

Audience's Attitudes: Does the writer view the audience as receptive, oppositional, or neutral?

Writer's Purpose: What is the writer's purpose for communicating to the audience?

Desired Action: What specific action(s) would the writer like the audience to take after reading the text?

Discursive Level

Institutions: What institutions are involved in sanctioning the communication? How do these institutions influence the communication at hand?

Subjectivities: What aspects of subjectivity (class, ethnicity, gender, sexuality, age, etc.) does the writer invoke in reference to the audience? Does the writer invoke these aspects of subjectivity in positive, negative, or neutral ways?

Cultural Values: Who are the ideal citizens of the community to which the writer belongs? What values do these citizens have in common?

Social Values: Who are the ideal citizens of the world outside the writer's community? What values does the writer impose on these citizens? How might these values differ from the real values held by the citizens outside the writer's own community?

Format, style, and genre focus on the textual invocation of the audience into a particular role (i.e., what Althusser calls "interpellation").

The writer's role, the audience's attitudes, the writer's purpose, and the desired action focus on the rhetorical relationship between the writer and audience. Institutions, subjectivities, and cultural and social values focus on the discursive context for communication. When applied to a particular document, the questions under each heading—the textual, rhetorical, and discursive levels—reveal more about the writing situation than analysis at just one of the levels can reveal.

The following letter was written by a student in a first-year composition class at East Carolina University. The assignment asked the student, whom I will call Bill Smith, to describe an "institutional" problem in a letter to someone who might be able to solve it.

Bill's Letter

---

321 Garrett Hall
East Carolina University
Greenville, NC 27858

November 7, 1997

Fred Rizzo, Director
Sanitation Department
East Carolina University
Greenville, NC 27858

Dear Mr. Rizzo:

I am writing you in regards to the uncleanness of the Garrett Hall restrooms. Lately, your crew has left our restrooms in a disgusting condition. I know that laziness will not be tolerated in your department, so I felt it necessary to bring my situation to your attention.

Your workers' attitudes of simply not caring have got to stop. Their laziness is forcing the people in my dorm, myself included, to use a restroom that could literally be condemned by the Health Department. The floors are wet and covered with urine, and the commodes are covered with used toilet paper, feces, and urine. This is unfair to everyone who uses these restrooms, including non-students.

I think you need to enforce a stricter schedule that ensures us of a clean restroom throughout the week, and not just on Mondays. Your workers need to get more done when they come, and they need to come more frequently. You may even find that all your workers need is a little more incentive to make them care a little more about our restrooms.

I have faith that you will discuss what I have said with your staff. I know that you want what is best for the students at East Carolina University. Thank you.

Sincerely,
Bill Smith
ECU Student

Let me begin by saying that there are many possible interpretations of Bill's letter based on the heuristic provided above; what follows are some of my own observations. At the textual level, Bill's letter calls his audience into a serious and formal role. Before reading the text, we see that Bill uses the "full block" letter format, which is typically reserved for "official" business. When we begin to read the text of the letter, we see Bill striving for a formal register with phrases such as "in regards to," "will not be tolerated," and "I felt it necessary." Continuing on, we find that Bill uses a problem-solution structure that invokes his audience into a position of authority. Through format, style, and genre, then, Bill attempts in this letter to place his reader into a role that commands respect and possesses the authority to solve Bill's problem. By most standards, Bill's letter is quite successful at the textual level of composing.

At the rhetorical level, Bill asserts himself even more directly. Throughout the letter, Bill adopts a two-part role: first, he is a Garrett Hall resident who is disgusted by the condition of the restrooms there; second, he is an ECU student, for whom Fred Rizzo wants "what is best." Bill views his audience as receptive to the problems and solutions he describes, since the director of sanitation would certainly take great care to insure the cleanliness of all restrooms on campus. Bill's purpose or desired action, then, is to encourage Fred Rizzo to create incentives that will combat the laziness of his workers. Bill has clearly thought about his own role and his audience's attitude toward the problem that he describes, and Bill's purpose is also clear. However, the degree of success the document might achieve could be questioned in a few ways. Mr. Rizzo, for example, probably has a friendly relationship with the people whom Bill calls lazy; thus, Mr. Rizzo may not receive the letter as positively as Bill might have initially thought. Also, Mr. Rizzo is probably a busy person, and his desire to please a few ECU students may be overstated. Overall, however, Bill has clearly considered several crucial aspects of his rhetorical situation, and these considerations guided his composing process.

When we move finally to the discursive level, Bill's letter begins to break down. In order to understand how ECU, qua institution, plays a role in the construction of this letter, I must first tell you something about the university. ECU is notorious for its "party school" reputation, and every freshman who enters ECU hears stories that reinforce this reputation. For example, each year, Playboy magazine runs a special section on the top party schools in the country. As the story goes, ECU had made the top of the list several years running, but then one year it was left off. At the bottom of the page, however, was the following notice: "no fair, East Carolina University—only amateurs are eligible." I have never seen this article, and I do not know anyone who has. It is quite possible that the story is not even true, or maybe it is—its verity is simply not relevant. The "Playboy story" is an integral part of ECU's lore, its mythology, and this story (as well as many others just like it) creates an institutional space within which new initiates (i.e., freshmen) construct their identities, and they are these very identities that impact ECU student writers' perceptions of their roles in many rhetorical situations. Bill's "ECU student" identity/subjectivity leads him to the impression that it is his right and the right of all ECU students to become so intoxicated that they cover the commodes with used toilet paper, feces, and urine. In Bill's letter, in other words, the students creating the mess are not only omitted from Bill's description of the problem, but they are even represented as victims of the sanitation workers' "laziness." Bill constructs "ECU students" as a community with a problem (filthy restrooms) and the sanitation workers as outsiders who cause the problem by not cleaning thoroughly or frequently enough, implying that ECU students, in the context of the university itself, are privileged to the point of absolute blamelessness. This identity construction and Bill's resulting rhetorical strategy require a remarkable disconnection between ECU students and their own excretions. When we examine Bill's letter from a discursive perspective, we see that Bill's rhetorical purpose might have been better served with a letter to members of his own community.

As we proceed through the three levels of composing, we find increasing problems with Bill's approach to his rhetorical situation, and the problems discovered through the discursive-level heuristic questions shed new light on the success or failure of Bill's letter at the rhetorical and textual levels. In his letter, for example, Bill constructs himself and all ECU students as members of a certain social class that is at least one level above the social class of the sanitation workers whom he criticizes. Since Fred Rizzo is Director of the Sanitation Department at ECU, it is probably safe to assume that he constructs his own social class identity more in connection to the workers in his department than he does in connection to the students whose bathrooms his workers clean. Thus, our explorations of this communicative situation at the discursive level reveal a class-based problem with Bill's consideration of audience, a problem that may not have surfaced had our explorations remained at the rhetorical level. Further, since Bill's discursive framework for the letter is potentially insulting to his audience, the formal language and problem-solution structure of the text might also strike Mr. Rizzo as particularly contemptuous, if not contradictory, calling him into a serious and formal role only to insult him and his co-workers.

These three levels of composing, textual, rhetorical, and discursive, are intricately interrelated, and success at any level requires success at all levels simultaneously. However, since, as I have pointed out, the textual and rhetorical levels of composing have received most of our attention in the history of composition, the remaining chapters in this book will focus most overtly on the discursive level, only occasionally touching explicitly on textual and rhetorical concerns. I hope my readers will understand, however, that one cannot consider the discursive level of composing without, at the very least, an implicit awareness of the textual and rhetorical qualities of discourse.

NOTES

1. See, for example, the responses to Hairston's article by John Trimbur, Robert Wood, Ron Strickland, William Thelin, William Rouster, and Toni Mester in CCC's May 1993 "Counterstatement" section (pages 248-57).

2. Linda Driskill points out that the Challenger disaster of 1986 occurred because Thiokol engineers, who had recognized a potential problem with the shuttle's O-rings, communicated their desire to delay the January 28 launch via "analogical reasoning," an invalid mode of communication in the context of NASA's "model-based logic" (139-42). Thiokol engineers, in other words, did not succeed in their communicative effort precisely because they lacked the discursive knowledge necessary to legitimate their warning, and the result was tragic. While few discursive misfires result in the loss of human life, many, I believe, can have serious economic, political, and social consequences for both author and community.

CHAPTER TWO

Social–Process
Rhetorical Inquiry

THERE IS MOUNTING EVIDENCE THAT COMPOSITION STUDIES HAS experienced a "social turn," and, according to John Trimbur, this social turn is the result of an increasing disaffection among certain composition teachers with the radical individualism implied by the early writing-as-process paradigm. In the mid-1980s, fueled by emerging debates about academic discourse, professional writing, and writing across the curriculum, scholars such as Patricia Bizzell, Lee Odell, and James Reither, among many others, began to question the individualism embedded in previous articulations of the writing process, arguing instead that different institutional contexts for writing (academic, professional, disciplinary) require different writing processes.[1] I believe that the best way to convey this contextual character of writing processes is to teach students the social nature and function of writing—both in the texts they produce for class and in those they encounter everyday outside of class.

In my experience, those who practice social approaches to composition studies expand the notion of the writing process from its current linear (and recursive) model to a cyclical model. In the linear model, the writing process begins with invention, progresses to revision, and ends with a final product. Of course, these stages in the process are recursive: we may decide during revision that we need to invent more details to support a weak argument, etc. But it is difficult, using this linear model of the writing process, to account for where topics and invented details come from and where essays go when they are finished—and to what effect. As David Bartholomae points out, "If writing is a process, it is also a product; and it is the product and not the plan for writing, that locates a writer on the page, that locates him in a text and a style and the codes and conventions that make both of them readable" (144). The recent interest among composition scholars in professional writing, writing across the curriculum, and academic discourse represents a renewed concern for written products (though no less concern for writing processes), especially insofar as they facilitate and constrain the production of texts, provide socio-discursive contexts for texts, and demand of writers a certain critical literacy as a precondition to entering ongoing conversations in any discourse community.

Thus, as an alternative to the linear (and recursive) process model currently in vogue, a model that I believe gives students the wrong idea about what happens when writers write, I propose a cyclical model of the writing process, one that accounts for the composing strategies of individual and collaborative writers as well as the socio-discursive lives of texts. And I represent this model in the form of a "*social-process*" heuristic for rhetorical inquiry based on the cycle of cultural production, contextual distribution, and critical consumption, a colligation of cultural studies methodologies for critiquing social institutions and cultural representations. Invention heuristics based on this cycle encourage students to understand language and culture as socially constructive forces (production) conditioned by contexts (distribution) and negotiated by critical subjectivities (consumption). Later in this chapter I will illustrate one such heuristic designed for use in an advertising analysis unit, perhaps the most common context for critical writing in cultural studies composition classes.

Through using the terms "cultural production," "contextual distribution," and "critical consumption," I intend both to invoke and transform the traditional Marxist concepts from which they derive. In his "Introduction to a Critique of Political Economy," Karl Marx describes the cycle of production, distribution, exchange, and consumption: "In the process of production, members of society appropriate (produce, fashion) natural products in accordance with human requirements; distribution determines the share the individual receives of these products; exchange supplies him with the particular products into which he wants to convert the portion accorded to him as a result of distribution; finally, in consumption the products become objects of use, i.e., they are appropriated by individuals" (193-94). And Marx completes the link in the cycle by arguing for a reciprocal understanding of production and consumption: "Production leads to consumption, for which it provides the material; consumption without production would have no object. But consumption also leads to production by providing for its products the subject for whom they are products" (196). Marx's own uses of the terms that I appropriate in this chapter ("production," "distribution," and "consumption") are, of course, decidedly modernist: production results in material goods; distribution and exchange refer to the portioning out of the produced goods and the money that *re*-presents them (in the modernist sense); and in consumption, subjects make use of the produced goods, possibly to produce other material goods, in turn creating a need for further production of the original products.

Postmodern cultural theory problematizes Marx's materialist description of the cycle of production, distribution, exchange, and consumption, opening up this useful heuristic to new interpretations and applications. In the postmodern age of mass production, material goods are, for the most part, no longer produced to satisfy the needs of consumers. Instead, goods exist as potentialities, and the real work of production is the creation of desire in consumers for the potentially producible goods; the physical production of goods becomes less important than the rhetorical construction of desire for them. Cultural production, then, is the creation of social values which manifest themselves in institutional practices and cultural artifacts. Within this postmodern framework, the distribution and exchange of material goods becomes secondary to the contextual distribution of the cultural values that construct desire in consumers.

Distribution, then, comprises the contexts of cultural values as they are manifest in particular institutional practices and cultural artifacts: some corporations, for example, serve as distributing contexts for particular personnel policies that perpetuate racist cultural values; and some magazines serve as distributing contexts for particular advertisements that perpetuate sexist cultural values. Critical consumption refers to the social uses to which "readers" put their interpretations of produced and distributed cultural values. Finally, the link that completes the cycle relies on the culturally productive power of critical consumption and the precondition of critical consumption for effective cultural production.

A few scholars in composition have adapted specific cultural studies methodologies for use as social-process guides to rhetorical inquiry, yet these few methodologies are limited in their theoretical and practical scope, engaging students in short-sighted concentration on just a single "moment" in the cycle of cultural production, contextual distribution, and critical consumption.

In "Composition and Cultural Studies," for example, James Berlin describes an invention heuristic for rhetorical inquiry based on cultural studies methodologies drawn primarily from Roland Barthes's work on advertising and John Fiske's work on television. In Berlin's composition classes, students generate critical essays about the production of cultural meaning in advertising using the following cultural studies heuristic for rhetorical inquiry:

> The major devices used to undertake this analysis [of advertisements] were three simple but powerful semiotic strategies that function as heuristics. The first of these is the location of binary oppositions in the texts—that is, the nature of the boundaries that give terms meaning. The second is the discovery of denotation and connotation as levels of meaning that involve contesting. The third is the reliance on invoking culturally specific narrative patterns—for example, the Horatio Alger myth or the Cinderella plot. These served as exploratory devices that enabled students to investigate semiotic codes as persuasive appeals, paying particular attention, once again, to the reliance of these codes on culturally specific categories of race, gender, and class. (51)

While Berlin's heuristic does draw on a number of established cultural studies methodologies, it does not encourage students to move beyond critiquing the production of cultural meaning in advertisements. Berlin's invention heuristic, particularly as it relates to advertising analysis, helps students gain a solid understanding of how texts produce certain social meanings. However, students using this heuristic are not encouraged to explore how the semiotic contexts of advertisements (the magazines, the television shows, etc.) condition the connotative meanings of key terms or how these contexts influence readers to invoke certain binary oppositions and social narratives over others; and students using this heuristic are not encouraged to formulate particular critical stances toward (or subject positions in relation to) the key terms, oppositions, and narratives they find represented in social institutions and cultural artifacts. Berlin's heuristic, in other words, leads only to "production criticism"—the examination of how cultural meaning is produced without concern for the semiotic force of its distributing context or the political force of critical consumption.

James Porter has also developed a heuristic that emphasizes a particular aspect of writing processes in cultural context. In *Audience and Rhetoric*, Porter describes his "forum analysis" heuristic as a method for exploring distributing contexts. Forum analysis offers a text-based alternative to the more common heuristics based on sociological ("real-reader") views of audience and community. Drawing primarily on Foucault's theory of discursive formations, Porter describes a "forum" as a "textual system" (106), a "concrete locale, a physical place for a discourse activity" (95); and forum analysis "assumes that audience is defined by the texts (oral and written) it produces and that the writer needs to systematically explore this textual field in order to produce acceptable discourse within it" (112). Porter's forum analysis heuristic has two main sections: under "background," students answer questions about the organizational affiliation, purpose, membership, origin, and reputation of the forum in question; and under "discourse conventions," students answer questions regarding who is allowed to speak or write in the forum, to whom they speak or write, what issues or topics are addressed in the forum, and in what form and style these issues are addressed (114-45). Forum analysis encourages writers to examine in detail the texts that constitute a particular discursive formation, and the knowledge gained through this brand of textual criticism is vital for rhetorical effectiveness. However, in isolation, forum analysis is incomplete; knowledge of the background and discourse conventions of a discursive formation does not necessarily enable a critical understanding of how cultural meaning is produced in particular texts, nor does it encourage participants in discursive formations to adopt critical subject positions in relation to particular discourses. Forum analysis teaches writers the importance of understanding the rhetorical flow of a discursive formation, but its short-sighted emphasis on distributing contexts leaves writers with an incomplete understanding of specific rhetorical practices used both in the production and consumption of texts.

Students who engage in detailed heuristic exploration of all three moments in the cycle of cultural production, contextual distribution, and critical consumption develop the sense that culture itself is a constantly changing process and that their own writing can influence some of the changes that cultures undergo, and social-process rhetorical inquiry brings these processes of rhetorical intervention consciously to bear on students' own critical writing. It is my goal in this chapter to develop a more complete social-process approach to composition than has previously been articulated.

THE CYCLE OF CULTURAL PRODUCTION, CONTEXTUAL DISTRIBUTION, AND CRITICAL CONSUMPTION

The cycle of cultural production, contextual distribution, and critical consumption has given rise to powerful writing in cultural studies, and I believe it holds similar potential to elicit powerful writing in response to cultural studies composition assignments. In "What Is Cultural Studies Anyway?" Richard Johnson, former director of the Birmingham Center for Contemporary Cultural Studies (BCCCS), describes the cycle of production, distribution, and consumption as a "heuristic" for understanding a wide variety of social phenomena, and this heuristic focuses attention on the complex interactions among encoders, texts, and decoders (all broadly defined) in the act of generating cultural meaning. The value of this cycle to composition studies is that, when viewed as a heuristic for rhetorical inquiry, it encourages students to understand both writing and culture as dialectical social processes through which they can derive a degree of agency. Cultural production, contextual distribution, and critical consumption represent three crucial "moments" in the process of developing social relations in lived cultures, and although I discuss each moment separately in the pages to come, a certain critical veracity is sacrificed if we lose sight of the cycle as a complete process. Each "moment," in other words, relies on the others for critical power and is indispensable to the cycle as a whole.

The first moment in the cycle isolates *cultural production* as the object of critical study. Studies of cultural production assume that social practices are conditioned by cultural values encoded into and decoded from texts. It is crucial, then, that students understand the ways in which encoders inscribe texts with "preferred readings," because as John Fiske points out, "the preferred reading *closes off* potential revolutionary meanings" (111) and conditions readers to adopt subject positions that fulfill the economic, political, and social desires of encoders. In the context of advertising, cultural production is the creation of the desire to consume, and this desire is achieved when advertisers promote certain preferred cultural values over others and associate their products with those values. Cultural values are produced through combinations of signs that function as associations, socialized links (often unconscious) between words and visual images and their subjective meanings, and they usually imply "ideal" consumer-audiences and social practices. Visual images in advertising signify associations between products and subjective desires. For example, most people associate stately mansions and expensive jewelry with upper class lifestyles; and when Liz Claiborne portrays mansions and jewelry in her perfume advertisements, the audience associates these products with their desire for wealth, and their consumption of Liz Claiborne perfume superficially and temporarily satisfies that desire. These associations between Liz Claiborne perfume and an upper class lifestyle imply a number of possible cultural values, one of which is: "Ideal wealthy women own mansions, diamonds, and Liz Claiborne perfume." Words in advertising also signify associations between products and subjective desires. For example, when the CEOs of the Coca-Cola corporation realized that New Coke was a failure, they changed back to its original recipe and advertised the new/old product as Coca-Cola Classic. The word "classic," of course, invokes images of the best things in life that have stood the test of time, and the Coca-Cola corporation wants its customers to associate this new/old "classic" product—actually the result of a disastrous marketing decision—with their nostalgic desire for the good old days when quality, not profit, was the top priority. The associations between Coca-Cola Classic and a desire for the uncomplicated past imply a number of possible cultural values, one of which is: "Ideal nostalgic cola consumers commemorate the past by drinking Coca-Cola Classic (instead of Pepsi, the choice of a new generation)." Images also function to limit the polysemy of meanings that words might invoke in readers (the word "dry" signifies different values when accompanied by images of deodorant or moisturizing cream), and words function to limit the polysemy of meanings that an image might invoke (the silhouette of a naked female figure signifies different values when accompanied by the words "sensual" or "natural"). These different kinds of associations in advertisements construct cultural values that encourage preferred readings, particular meanings that encoding advertisers want decoding consumers to attribute to the advertised products.

Most advertising cultural values construct readers as ideal identities and encourage certain ideal social practices over others, and they relate these ideal practices to particular products. Cultural values have the surface appearance of descriptive statements; however, they operate culturally as prescriptive behavioral directives that position readers within certain advantageous subjectivities: "if *you* want to be an ideal progressive young adult, then you *should* drink Zima malt beverage," or "if *you* want to be an ideal rugged man, then you *should* smoke Marlboro cigarettes." The element missing from cultural values is the reason for which particular ideal practices are favored over others; the motives that generate cultural values are often selfish and work against the best interests of many people whose lives they influence. For example, cultural values in advertisements for expensive products are often directed toward middle and low income families who cannot reasonably afford the advertised merchandise—e.g., Nike ads selling the dream of escaping ghettos through sports, and state lottery ads selling the dream of financial security through "sure thing" odds. Although cultural values are inevitable and essential aspects of any social arrangement, the ones that result in marginalizing and oppressive cultural practices can be recognized through critical reading and revised through careful rhetorical interventions into the institutions and artifacts that construct and maintain these values. This is one goal that students strive to achieve in advertising analysis essays. Yet it is naive to assume that texts such as advertisements—in and of themselves—contain pure meaning and that readers consume this meaning through direct and uncritical identification with the texts. We cannot, therefore, revise cultural values until we understand their modes of contextual distribution and critical consumption as well.

The second moment in the cycle isolates *contextual distribution* as the object of critical study. It is important to examine the distributing contexts of cultural values because, as Johnson points out, "context is crucial to the production of meaning" (62). When we critique a distributing medium, we examine "the subjective or cultural forms which it realizes and makes available" (62). In advertising, then, contextual distribution is the location (the specific magazine, television show, radio program, etc.) in which the cultural values of particular ads are presented to potential consumer audiences, and this location further limits the polysemy of meanings that advertisements might invoke. Media contexts construct their own cultural values through associations, socialized links between recurring key words, hot topics, and visual images and their subjective meanings, and they usually imply "ideal" audiences and social practices. Every element of every magazine contributes to the construction of associations—the cover design, table of contents, editorials, letters to the editor, regular columns, feature articles and their accompanying photographs, personals, and advertisements, etc. Associations link magazines with preferred readings and cultural values, some of which may conflict—popular magazines rarely represent a monolithic discourse. In *Esquire*, for example, certain key words (media, fashion), hot topics (electronic gadgets, Armani), and prominent visual images (handsome single men wearing designer casual suits) construct subjective desires in young men for financial excess and casual European good looks, which imply a number of possible cultural values: "ideal young men own the latest technologies and understand their (elitist) social significance," and "ideal young men wear designer clothes for confidence and comfort (not necessarily for romantic purposes)." Through associations, distributing media promote certain cultural values over others, and these values either support or subvert the cultural values in the advertisements they contain. For example, the predominant cultural values in *Self* magazine—e.g., "ideal healthy women enjoy active lifestyles achieved through safe exercise and nutritional diets"—both subvert a Baileys Light ad (alcohol slows human metabolism making exercise difficult and often leading to weight gain) and also support it (Baileys Light has 33% fewer calories and 50% less fat than Baileys Irish Cream, so it is a healthier option when you want to relax with a drink).

As Johnson points out, "narratives or images always imply or construct a position or positions from which they are to be read or viewed," and certain media—popular magazines in particular—"naturalize the means by which [subject] positioning is achieved." The purpose of cultural studies is to render these processes of subject positioning "hitherto unconsciously suffered (and enjoyed) open to explicit analysis" (66). In their advertising analysis essays, students critique the subject positioning engaged in by the medium that distributes the advertisement they have chosen as the focus of their critical essays, and they compare and contrast the cultural values in their advertisement with the values in its distributing medium, looking specifically for consistencies and contradictions.

The third moment in the cycle isolates *critical consumption* as the object of study. Here the focus turns from the cultural values produced in texts and their distributing media to the subjectivities who encounter the produced and distributed values. When we study consumption, we study the impact media messages have on us as "readers." While Johnson acknowledges the powers distributing media have to construct subject positions for their readers, he is careful to point out that readers also possess the powerful agency to construct alternative narratives and images: "human beings and social movements also strive to produce some coherence and continuity, and through this, exercise some control over feelings, conditions and destinies" (69). And this control is achieved through "critique," which "involves stealing away the more useful elements [of media cultures] and rejecting the rest" (38). Critical analysis helps students problematize the subject positions constructed for them in texts, and cultural studies writing assignments encourage students to exert pressure on the construction of their own subject positions from which they might solve social problems for the benefit of communities.

In "Encoding/Decoding," Stuart Hall, also former director of the BCCCS, argues that media generate meaning using a "dominant hegemonic" code, a metalanguage that inherently promotes the cultural values of those already in power; and media texts are encoded with preferred readings (selected from the dominant hegemonic code) that construct subject positions for consumers of media messages.[2] As Dave Morley points out, "texts privilege a certain reading in part by inscribing certain preferred discursive positions from which its discourse appears 'natural,' transparently aligned to 'the real' and credible" (167). Uncritical audiences accommodate preferred readings, and they adopt subject positions constructed for them in media by dominant groups. The cultural values inscribed in media representations appear to these audiences as universal truths, inscribed in nature, beyond the realm of critical questioning. Although advertisements and their distributing contexts do at times promote positive cultural values (e.g., many of the new computer animated Levi's ads suggest that ideal women are independent and creative), too often as readers we accommodate marginalizing values uncritically and accept them as objective facts. When we accommodate cultural values without interrogating them, we allow the media that perpetuate these values to interpret our worlds for us, and we accept their interpretations without questioning the often self-serving social motives implicit in their assumptions. However, as Lawrence Grossberg argues, "the fact that texts encode certain preferred readings does not guarantee that they are read accordingly; that is, we cannot assume effects simply from origins" (138); and Morley agrees that a preferred reading "cannot be the only reading inscribed in the text, and it certainly cannot be the only reading which different readers can make of it" (167).

Some communities, often sub-cultures, establish what Hall refers to as "oppositional" codes, metalanguages that inherently resist the hegemonic cultural values of those in power; and media texts, encoded with "dominant" preferred readings, are rejected for promoting values that contradict those of the interpreting community. Based on oppositional codes, audiences deliberately decode media representations according to resistant logics. Audiences resist cultural values when they consciously understand the underlying messages in advertisements and their distributing contexts, yet they refuse to accept the cultural implications of these values and messages. From an "oppositional" perspective, media messages are perceived as "dominant" and therefore oppressive, and they are consumed according to (often marginalized) counter-cultural logics which subvert the dominant hegemonic code. Environmentalists, for example, may consume dominant cultural values in advertisements extolling the convenience, comfort, and economy of disposable diapers through oppositional codes, arguing instead that convenience, comfort, and economy are poor excuses for the systematic destruction of entire ecosystems. But resistance from oppositional subject positions can lead to reactionary rhetorical practices; and oppositional rhetoric elicits oppositional audience responses that often smother the potential for social change.

Most decoding operates according to "negotiated" codes, metalanguages that take the place of the dominant hegemonic code when it is unable to account for situated cultural values. Negotiated codes are not oppositional; they function as contingent correctives to the dominant hegemonic code when dominant cultural values no longer serve the socio-political interests of certain populations. We negotiate cultural codes in advertisements when we invoke specific circumstances from our own social experiences to which the dominant cultural values in advertisements do not necessarily apply, and this act of negotiation may affect our desire for—and use of—the advertised products. Some working class families, for example, may negotiate ads for Fancy Feast cat food, accommodating the desire for a comfortable lifestyle but resisting Fancy Feast's promotion of excessive consumption for its own sake. Some women may negotiate ads for Revlon Fire and Ice perfume, accommodating their desire for feminine sensuality while resisting Revlon's implication, in their use of anorexic models, that the ideal female body is thin. Some African Americans may negotiate ads for Lustrasilk Luxury Care relaxing cream, accommodating the desire for straight hair yet resisting Lustrasilk's representations of ethnic neutrality—the models pictured in the ad have light brown skin—by styling their hair in distinctively Afrocentric fashions. As Elizabeth Ellsworth points out, negotiation requires audiences who "are not passive recipients of the communications of others. Rather, they actively, and unpredictably, construct diverse and sometimes contradictory meanings for the same text" (61). And audiences' individual and collective cultural experiences generate these divergent readings. According to Morley, "At the moment of textual encounter other discourses are always in play other than those of the particular text in focus—discourses which depend on other discursive formations, brought into play by the subject's placing in other practices—cultural, educational, institutional" (163). These "other practices" account for divergent negotiations of advertisements, and they comprise the predominant critical focus of advertising analysis essays.

Johnson and others theorize cultural production, contextual distribution, and critical consumption as a *cyclical process*, necessitating a forward-looking link between critical consumption and the future production, distribution, and consumption of cultural values. The cultural production, contextual distribution, and critical consumption of cultural values in all new texts change, in different ways and to varying degrees, the character of the cultures (and the individuals within the cultures) that consume them, and each instance of critical consumption generates new exigencies for different styles of production, distribution, and consumption; as cultures change with the accommodation, resistance, and negotiation of cultural values represented in texts, new economic, social, and political values arise, requiring new texts to address emergent cultural needs. It is in this link between critical consumption and the future production, distribution, and consumption of cultural values where composition studies lends practical effectivity to cultural studies, which remains primarily an academic discourse. Specific concerns in rhetoric and composition for matters of audience, purpose, and style illuminate the importance of practical rhetorical interventions based on the critical knowledge gained through advertising analysis. Thus, while cultural studies is indeed "an alchemy for producing useful knowledge" (Johnson 38) derived through critical consumption, composition studies is a process for transforming "useful knowledge" into *shared knowledge* that influences the future production, distribution, and consumption of cultural values. Critical consumption alone does not, in and of itself, lead to social reform; only careful rhetorical interventions into this cycle make possible the reforms that cultural studies seeks.

In the context of the advertising analysis assignment that I describe in Appendix A, students create links between their critical consumption of advertisements and the future production, distribution, and consumption of cultural values by writing letters that attempt to solve some of the problems they discover in their heuristic inquiries and describe in their critical essays, and they direct their letters to *at least* one of three possible audiences: representatives of the company that either makes the product or offers the service advertised (cultural production audience); editors of the magazine that distributes the advertisement (contextual distribution audience); and/or consumers who encounter the advertisement or its distributing medium on a regular basis (critical consumption audience). Before writing these letters, students consider the *quantity of knowledge* each audience might have regarding the cultural values promoted in the advertisement, and the *quality of attitude* each audience might have toward potential reform in the future production, distribution, and/or consumption of the cultural values promoted in the advertisement. These two considerations are crucial to the success of the letters, since they determine students' rhetorical aims (informative when audiences know little and/or have positive attitudes toward reform, and persuasive when audiences know much and/or are resistant toward reform; most of the letters, however, contain mixtures of informative and persuasive discourse). Having explored the knowledge and attitudes of each audience, students then decide which audience(s) would, having received an effective letter, most likely influence the future production, distribution, and consumption of cultural values within the context of the advertisement in question. This process of rhetorical intervention into the cycle of cultural production, contextual distribution, and critical consumption transforms "useful knowledge" into shared knowledge and enhances the potential for social change, change that is less likely to occur if students end their composing processes with critical essays.

Extensive heuristic exploration of *all three* "moments" in the cycle of cultural production, contextual distribution, and critical consumption—and, most importantly, rhetorical intervention into the cycle (in the link between critical consumption and the future production, distribution, and consumption of cultural values)—is crucial to the practice of social-process rhetorical inquiry. Heuristics that foreground only one of these moments, as Johnson points out, apply only to "those parts of the process which they have most clearly in view," and these heuristics, like the ones described by Berlin and Porter, are "incomplete, liable to mislead, in that they are only partial, and therefore cannot grasp the process as a whole" (Johnson, 46). This "process," of course, is the cycle of developing social relations that cultural studies seeks to critique, and unbalanced attention to just one moment in this process leads to short-sighted conclusions which may inhibit the potential for political action. Social-process rhetorical inquiry incorporates *all three* moments in the cycle of cultural production, contextual distribution, and critical consumption into focused and balanced heuristic exploration of the entire process of developing social relations.

SOCIAL-PROCESS RHETORICAL INQUIRY

In Appendix A, I present an advertising analysis assignment with two parts, a critical essay and a practical letter. This assignment is intentionally abstract, since students will develop their own responses as they engage the invention heuristic in Appendix B. As the assignment suggests, students should first choose a magazine with which they are familiar; it helps if they already know the "code(s)" from which the magazine draws. I encourage students to select magazines with clear audiences, such as *Seventeen, GQ, Rolling Stone, Self, Muscle, Hot Rod,* etc. Magazines like *Newsweek, Time, Us,* and *People* are indeed directed at certain kinds of readers, but because they target broad audiences they tend to draw from a number of divergent "codes," which can confuse students in their critiques of the cultural values in media. Once students have chosen a magazine for the assignment, I ask them to read it cover-to-cover, paying careful attention to everything: the cover design, table of contents, editorials, letters to the editor, regular columns, feature articles and their accompanying photographs, personals, and, of course, advertisements. As they read, students look specifically for recurring key words, hot topics, and prominent visual images that associate the magazine with certain preferred readings and cultural values. The goal here is to give students a "total experience" with the magazine, not just a selective experience with a few articles and ads. Once students have oriented themselves to the "code(s)" within which the magazine operates, their task is to select one advertisement from the magazine; this ad will become the focus of their critical and practical essays. Selecting a good ad is crucial since not all are equally right for the assignment. The best advertisements have a fairly balanced mixture of visual images and written text that promote cultural values. Ads that are unbalanced toward either visual or textual representations do not highlight the *interaction* of these elements in the construction of cultural values.

While students are reading their magazines and selecting an ad for their critical essays, I spend two class periods helping students apply the heuristic in Appendix B to a specific magazine and a few of its advertisements. Since this magazine and its ads are the objects of class discussion, they are then off limits for the students' advertising analysis essays. During the first class period, I bring in several (as needed) identical copies of a single magazine with a well defined audience. I have students examine the magazine issues in groups, working through the "contextual distribution" questions in the Appendix B heuristic. I give student groups about thirty minutes to examine every aspect of the magazine, after which we discuss the associations and values promoted in the medium. During our class discussion of the magazine, I have students generate lists (which I write on the chalk board) of the recurring key words, hot topics, and prominent visual images. We usually fill the chalk board with words, topics, and images, some of which may contradict others in the lists, serving to demonstrate the polysemous codes within which magazines operate. Having filled the chalk board with lists, students then generate the subjective meanings and desires that the recurring key words, hot topics, and prominent visual images in the magazine imply. If there is enough room on the chalk board, I try to write the meanings and desires below our lists of words, topics, and images so that students can clearly see their interrelationships.

Students then generate cultural values implied in the magazine, and I take this classroom opportunity to discuss what makes a good statement of cultural value. Effective statements of cultural value have two components: ideal identities and ideal social practices. First students ask from the perspective of the magazine in question, "What ideal identities do the key words, hot topics, and visual images in the magazine construct?" As we have seen, the key words, topics, and images in *Esquire* construct "young men" as its ideal audience, and the key words, topics, and images in *Self* construct "healthy women" as its ideal audience. Some magazines may construct two or three different identities. Next students ask, again from the perspective of the magazine, "What ideal social practices do the key words, hot topics, and visual images in the magazine construct for that ideal audience?" The key words, topics, and images in *Esquire* construct purchasing high tech gadgets and designer clothing as ideal social practices for young men, and the key words, topics, and images in *Self* construct safe exercise and dieting as ideal social practices for healthy women. Most magazines construct multiple ideal social practices for their ideal audience(s). We then consider the relevant questions from the "critical consumption" section of the heuristic in Appendix B, critiquing each cultural value (arguing for our accommodation, resistance, and/or negotiation of it) and its association with the magazine under examination.

During the second class period, while students are reading their magazines and selecting an ad for their critical and practical essays, I have students collaboratively choose two or three ads from the magazines we examined during the previous class period. Here we discuss the differences between balanced and unbalanced ads, and the class votes on which few they would like to critique for the rest of the class period. With the ads chosen, and examining them one at a time, students begin to generate lists of associations among the words and images in the ads and the subjective desires they imply. Again, I write these lists of associations on the chalk board so that students can look at them as they begin to formulate the statements of cultural value implied by the associations. In formulating these statements of cultural value, first students must ask from the perspective of each advertisement in question, "What ideal identities do the words and visual images in the ad construct?" In IBM laptop computer ads, for example, words and images imply that ideal consumers are successful CEOs; in Calvin Klein jeans ads, ideal consumers are sexy women; and in Gerber baby food ads, ideal consumers are doting mothers. Some ads may construct two or three different ideal identities. Next students ask from the perspective of the advertisement, "What ideal social practices do the words and visual images in the ad construct for that ideal audience?" IBM's ideal successful CEOs work late hours on (IBM) laptop computers; Calvin Klein's ideal sexy women wear close-fitting (Calvin Klein) jeans; and Gerber's ideal doting mothers stay home with their kids and feed them (Gerber) baby foods. Some ads may also construct multiple ideal social practices for their ideal audience(s). We then consider the relevant questions from the "critical consumption" section of the heuristic in Appendix B, critiquing each cultural value (arguing for our accommodation, resistance, and/or negotiation of it) and its association with the advertised product.

We end this second class period exploring each potential audience for our own rhetorical interventions into the cycle of cultural production, contextual distribution, and critical consumption. For example, students might decide to write a letter to IBM executives explaining that their advertisements encourage husbands and fathers to neglect their families, which could be damaging to IBM's long-term public reputation, and recommending that they discuss a different promotional campaign with their advertising department. Students might write a letter to the editors of *Esquire* magazine, a medium that distributes the IBM advertisement, explaining that the ad contradicts *Esquire*'s values regarding casual lifestyles, and recommending that they discontinue the ad in future issues. Finally, students might write a letter to *Consumer Reports* magazine (or a local newspaper for a local ad) describing to other potential consumers the damaging cultural values promoted in IBM advertisements, and recommending that consumers boycott IBM products until it changes its advertising practices. In most instances, a three letter combination is the best rhetorical choice for enacting changes in product/service advertising. However, there are audiences that will decode such letters oppositionally; often, in these cases, sending just one or two letters to potentially receptive audiences is the best rhetorical choice. "Potential impact" is an important consideration in students' choice of audiences. I always encourage students to send their letters to the audiences they most want to reach, and we discuss the responses as they arrive throughout the rest of the semester. Many of the responses are oppositional and reactionary, and students learn quite a bit about tone and purpose from critiquing them; they also learn valuable political lessons about the effectiveness or ineffectiveness of their own rhetorical choices. Other responses, however, acknowledge the problems students have pointed out in their letters, describing a potential course of action, and the students take pride in knowing that their writing has affected for the better their own cultural lives and the lives of others.

This kind of hands-on classroom practice gives students the confidence they need to fully engage the difficult heuristic questions in Appendix B, and individual teachers may spend more or less class time on heuristic exploration as the need arises. It is crucial for a social-process approach to rhetorical inquiry that students engage the heuristic cycle of cultural production, contextual distribution, and critical consumption *collaboratively,* since students working in isolation may: 1) view advertisements and their distributing media as monolithic, true, universal representations, leaving accommodation as the only viable critical stance; or 2) view advertisements and their distributing media as monolithic, false, particularized representations, leaving resistance as the only viable critical stance. Collaborative heuristic inquiry, on the other hand, highlights the plurality of cultural values promoted in advertisements and their distributing media; in class, students argue among themselves about what cultural values advertisements and magazines represent, and they argue even more about their own negotiations of these cultural values. Even when teachers assign the advertising analysis critical and practical essays as individual projects, initial collaborative heuristic inquiry demonstrates to students the polysemous discourses represented in the advertisements and magazines they will critique, and this knowledge results, I believe, in more complicated critical writing than when students do not collaborate.

The advertising analysis assignment works best when it is preceded with collaborative heuristic inquiry, but it is most successful, in my own experience, when the entire assignment is written collaboratively by groups of three or four students. Here social-process rhetorical inquiry is best served because students must reconcile their differences (many of which are left graphically represented in the critical essay as dialogue) into a single rhetorical purpose in the practical essays. Collaborative heuristic inquiry into the cycle of cultural production, contextual distribution, and critical consumption generates polysemous readings of ads and magazines; however, this polysemy must be constrained if students' rhetorical interventions are to succeed.

The advertising analysis assignment I describe also works equally well with or without research. Students can use research in a number of ways in critical essays and rhetorical interventions to improve their skills in conducting primary and secondary research and incorporating sources into their writing. Under "cultural production," for example, students might find print sources on the company that makes the product or offers the service: they might, for example, research the Philip Morris company to explore its own cultural values as a tobacco company and to what extent those values are manifested in their ads for Marlboro cigarettes. Under "contextual distribution," students might find print sources on the company that owns and distributes the magazine that contains the ad in question: they might, for example, research Condé Nast Publications to explore its own cultural values as a communications corporation and to what extent those values are manifested in the pages of *Glamour* magazine. Under "critical consumption," students might interview different populations regarding their reactions to the cultural values promoted in the advertisement or magazine in question. Here students might gather and record reactions from "cultural groups" to their advertisement: they might explore a variety of responses from different ethnicities, social classes, genders, sexual preferences, religions, political affiliations, educational backgrounds, geographical regions, etc. These different responses, like the earlier collaborative heuristic explorations, complicate critical consumption by highlighting the polysemous character of cultural values, and they foster a more inclusive ethic in students' critical writing.

The cultural studies methodology for rhetorical invention described in Appendix B is a *social-process* heuristic precisely because of its cyclical character. Not only does it encourage students to understand writing as a process, but it also encourages students to understand culture itself as a process that is open to change through careful rhetorical intervention. The heuristic gains its most significant power when students critically consume the production and distribution of cultural values with an eye toward producing their own values to be distributed and consumed in particular discourse communities. In other words, once students have examined an advertisement in terms of its production of cultural values and its distribution in a semiotic context, and they have explored their own critical consumption of the produced values in both the ad and its context, then they must continue the cycle through specific rhetorical interventions into the processes of developing social relations—they must produce texts of their own for specific distributing contexts and for consumption within particular communities, which in turn elicit further texts, contexts, and critical readings, etc. And these rhetorical interventions are most effective when cultural values have been negotiated through dialectical rhetorical practices that incorporate multiple perspectives on social problems.

I propose a movement in writing instruction toward what I have called *social-process* rhetorical inquiry, and this movement requires further pedagogical adaptations of social theory and cultural studies methodologies into invention heuristics for critical inquiry. These heuristics, however, should provide students with guidelines for careful rhetorical inquiry through the complete cycle of cultural production, contextual distribution, and critical consumption, and they should help students explore means for rhetorical interventions into this cycle. Invention heuristics for critical inquiry based on social theory and cultural studies methodologies help student writers tap into the knowledge they already possess about their own cultural experience, thereby demystifying critical writing for many students who might otherwise precipitously adopt "oppositional" perspectives in relation to cultural studies composition pedagogies.

NOTES

1. I have in mind Odell's "Beyond the Text: Relations between Writing and Social Context" (1985), and Reither's "Writing and Knowing:

Toward Redefining the Writing Process" (1985), and several of the articles from the 1980s that are collected in Bizzell's *Academic Discourse and Critical Consciousness*.

2. It is important to note, however, that a dominant hegemonic code is only dominant from a particular perspective; in other words, what is dominant in one social arrangement or discursive formation (environmentalist codes in Democratic discourse on preserving the environment) may be marginalized in another social arrangement or discursive formation (environmentalist codes in Republican discourse on reducing government excess). Unfortunately, much cultural studies still theorizes media as a monolithic discourse, encoding a single "dominant" ideological perspective into all media messages, and it still theorizes media audiences as the duped "masses." While such theories, developed in the 1940s and 1950s by members of the Frankfurt Institute for Social Research, helped explain Nazi crimes against humanity, these totalizing theories are overly simplistic when applied to the complex polysemy characteristic of postmodern media.

Advertising Critical and Practical Essays: Assignments

In this essay, you will examine the culture of "advertising" critically. We all encounter hundreds of advertisements every single day, whether we are conscious of them or not. Advertisements bombard us in our cars, at work, at school, and—most of all—in our homes during leisure time. It is crucial, therefore, that we develop a critical understanding of how advertisements affect us and our surroundings. Only then do we have the power to choose consciously whether to accommodate, resist, or negotiate the cultural values each advertisement promotes.

Your first task in this assignment is to choose a magazine with which you are already familiar, and get a recent copy of it (you will turn the copy in when you turn in your final advertising critical and practical essays). Next, choose an advertisement within the particular magazine issue you have bought or borrowed; it should have an equal mixture of visual and verbal elements. This advertisement will be the primary focus of your critical and practical essays.

The Critical Essay

You have two options for the general structure of your advertising critical essay: 1) you might organize your critique around the concepts in the invention, slightly altering their order to contextual distribution, cultural production, and critical consumption; or 2) you might organize your critique around the dominant cultural values that you find in the advertisement and the magazine.

The Practical Letter

Attempt to resolve one or two problems that you describe in your critical essay by writing at least one formal letter for which there are three possible audiences and purposes:

- a letter to the company that makes the product or offers the service advertised, providing specific and viable alternatives to their present advertising practices.
- a letter to the editors of the advertisement's distributing medium, pointing out contradictions between the medium and the advertisement it contains.
- a letter to the editors of *Consumer Reports* magazine, warning other potential consumers about the advertising practices of the company and/or medium in question.

*The Cycle of Cultural Production, Contextual
Distribution, and Critical Consumption:
A Cultural Studies Heuristic for Rhetorical Inquiry into Advertising*

This heuristic is designed to help you explore the cycle of cultural production, contextual distribution, and critical consumption as it relates to magazine advertisements.

Cultural Production

Explore the advertisement's production of cultural values ("ideal" audiences and social practices) through associations:

- List associations between the predominant images in the advertisement and their subjective meanings.
- List associations between the key words in the advertisement and their subjective meanings.
- What cultural values do the associations in the advertisement imply?
- Circle the cultural values with which you feel uncomfortable.

Contextual Distribution

Explore the cultural values of the magazine that distributes the advertisement you have chosen to critique:

- List associations between the key words in the magazine and their subjective meanings.
- List associations between the hot topics in the magazine and their subjective meanings.
- List associations between the predominant visual images in the magazine and their subjective meanings.
- What cultural values do the associations in the magazine imply?
- Mark with an asterisk the cultural values of the magazine that directly contradict the cultural values of the advertisement.
- Circle the cultural values of the magazine with which you feel uncomfortable.

Critical Consumption

Critique (accommodate, resist, and, most importantly, negotiate) the cultural values in the advertisement and its distributing medium:

- Identify cultural values in the advertisement and the magazine that you accommodate, and explain based on your own personal experience why you accommodate those values.
- In the case of each cultural value that you accommodate in the advertisement, explain whether or not you believe the value is legitimately associated with the advertised product.
- Identify cultural values in the advertisement and the magazine that you resist, and explain based on your own personal experience why you resist those values.
- In the case of each cultural value that you resist in the advertisement, explain whether or not you believe the value is legitimately associated with the advertised product.
- Identify cultural values in the advertisement and the magazine that you negotiate, and explain based on your own personal experience why you negotiate those values.
- In the case of each cultural value that you negotiate in the advertisement, explain whether or not you believe the value is legitimately associated with the advertised product.

Rhetorical Intervention as Cultural Production

Compose effective rhetorical documents challenging the cultural values that do not serve the interests of a community to which you belong:

Cultural Production Audience

- Do representatives of the company (that either makes the product or offers the service) know that the cultural values in their advertisement have negative effects on you and other consumers?
- What is the company's attitude toward these negative effects?

Contextual Distribution Audience

- Do the editors of the magazine know that the cultural values in the advertisement contradict the cultural values of their medium?
- What is the editors' attitude toward these contradictions?

Critical Consumption Audience

- Do other consumers know that the cultural values in the advertisement and/or the magazine have negative effects on them?
- What are consumers' attitudes toward these negative effects?

The Post–Process Movement in Composition Studies

THE TERM *POST-PROCESS* HAS GAINED SOME CURRENCY IN COMPOSI-
tion studies, yet its meaning remains unclear. Reactions among writing teachers to the term post-process are often as strong as reactions
have been among literary theorists to the term postmodern. One of
the reasons for such reactions to these terms is that in each idiomatic
usage the "post" means something different, ranging anywhere from
a "radical rejection" to a "complex extension" of what came before. In
this chapter, I argue that the most fruitful meaning for the "post" in
post-process is "extension," not "rejection," and I offer social-process
rhetorical inquiry as a pedagogical method for extending our present
view of the composing process into the social world of discourse.

THE WRITING PROCESS MOVEMENT[1]

As Lester Faigley, James Berlin, and others have argued, the
1960s and 1970s ushered in a new historical moment in composition
studies, a moment marked by social revolution and educational
reform. During these foundational decades, writing teachers as
diverse as Peter Elbow, Janet Emig, Janice Lauer, Richard Young,
and many others began to examine carefully and act upon Donald
Murray's famous call to educational arms, "Teach Writing as a
Process not Product."[2] Reacting against the rigid rules that governed
student writing before the Vietnam War, these disparate scholars all
agreed that the best way to teach writing was to throw away

mode-based literary and non-fiction readers (which functioned as illusive manifestations of our grading standards) and focus instead on what happens when individuals write, and they defined their own educational space in opposition to the space occupied by current-traditional rhetoric.

During its tenure in college composition studies, the writing process movement shifted from a negative dialectic against the evils of current-traditional rhetoric to a more positive articulation of its own goals and strategies. And in this shift, the writing process movement became more and more associated with expressivist approaches to teaching composition. Lad Tobin, for example, suggests, "Though there is not a necessary connection between process pedagogy and personal writing, . . . the two have often been linked in practice and perception" (6), and Robert Yagelski laments that the terms "process" and "expressivism" are often used synonymously (206). Throughout the 1970s and 1980s, this burgeoning expressivist writing process movement took hold of the college composition studies scene and became the "standard" for effective writing instruction, especially at certain influential institutions such as the University of Massachusetts and the University of New Hampshire. Through a variety of invention strategies (freewriting, clustering, journaling, brainstorming, etc.), students accessed their inner speech, harnessed the multiplicities of meanings that they found within themselves beyond the limiting confines of institutional discourses; and through re-vision, students were encouraged to look and look again at their own identities in a variety of personalized contexts.

This is not to say, of course, that approaches to writing instruction other than expressivism did not exist in the 1970s and 1980s. They did. But many, such as those arising out of cognitive psychology, were co-opted by expressivism, and with very little effort indeed. Most of us would acknowledge that the early rhetoric of cognitive psychology, articulated in landmark studies by Janet Emig and Linda Flower, among others, is "transactional" (to borrow a term from James Berlin's *Rhetoric and Reality*), engaging more than one element in the traditional rhetorical triangle. In this respect, cognitivist rhetorics are distinct from mostly subjective rhetorics such as expressivism. Yet these early cognitivist rhetorics, despite having certain transactional qualities, still focused on the "psychology of the individual" (Berlin, *Rhetoric and Reality* 159). For example, while Linda Flower recommended that writers convert writer-based prose into reader-based prose (a transactional move), she still encouraged novice students to begin with writer-based prose—advice Peter Elbow would also give in "Closing My Eyes as I Speak" a few years after Flower's landmark essays on cognitive problem solving. It was easy, really: expressivists simply used Flower's innovative strategies for inventing writer-based prose, and they stopped there.

But all of this has been utterly problematized in the 1990s. In *The Construction of Negotiated Meaning,* for example, Flower articulates a "social-cognitive" approach to literacy and composing, negotiating in the process a position between expressivist and social epistemic rhetoric. Although Flower admits, "I guess I am a bit of a conventionalist, brought up on the language of expressive writing" (293), she nevertheless seeks "an integrated vision of literacy that recognizes that writers need to know discourse conventions as well as strategies, to belong to a community and still take independent journeys of the mind" (292). This kind of negotiation articulates an aporia between traditional oppositions such as social versus cognitivist approaches to teaching writing. And it is just this sort of impulse to negotiate that I believe forms both the theoretical and pragmatic foundation of a "post-process" composition studies that extends (rather than rejects) its own history.

POST-PROCESS COMPOSITION: *Rejecting* THE WRITING PROCESS MOVEMENT

Let me begin my discussion of the recent "post" responses to the writing process movement with a conception of post-process composition that I believe has limited value in classroom practice, i.e., the idea that the post-process movement constitutes a radical break with the concerns of the writing process movement. Thomas Kent, the foremost advocate of this *"anti*-process" version of post-process composition, argues against what he calls "systemic rhetoric" which "treats discourse production and discourse analysis as codifiable processes" ("Beyond" 492). In composition studies, Kent describes three different manifestations of systemic rhetoric—expressivist, empirical, and social constructionist—that, though different in some ways, all "assume that discourse production and analysis can be reduced to systemic processes and taught in classrooms in some codified manner" ("Paralogic" 25). Kent argues, however, that "discourse production and analysis refute systematization," and so "we cannot codify our interpretive acts and then arrange them in any sort of systemic metalanguage" (35). Thus, Kent continues, "With this process approach to writing instruction, . . . we assume that the writer can discover, in some predictable way, what it is she wants to say and how to say it: we mistakenly assume that a fit, link, or convention exists between the different hermeneutic strategies employed by both the writer and the reader" (36). Writing, then, is not a codified process of discovering ideas but a hermeneutic exploration of different interpretive strategies, and writing teachers, then, become paralogic participants in a classroom dialogue rather than masters of some desired discourse (37).

While I agree with Kent that language is much too unstable to be codified into *universal* principles for generating discourse, I do not believe that this is what the writing process movement in composition has done. Language, as Kent describes it, is inherently unstable and fraught with contradiction, and on this point I concur. However, invention and revision strategies, as I understand and teach them, do not assume a stable and predictable linguistic system for generating universal meaning; their function is, instead, to harness the polyphonic character of language in communities, to develop rather than constrict a writer's sense of purpose. When I teach my composition students about language, I tell them that it is unstable, that meaning resides in the communication context and in each person's interpretation of the very words we use. But I also tell them that *writing* well transforms this unstable language into discourse that can accomplish real purposes. And while we cannot with absolute certainty predict the hermeneutic strategies readers might use in the interpretation of a text, the writer of that text can, I believe, invoke in a reader certain hermeneutic strategies over others. Just as an audience might be invoked into particular relational roles by the linguistic qualities of a text, so too can readers be invoked into particular interpretive stances by the linguistic qualities of a text. We have, of course, learned this lesson well from Walter Ong, Douglas Park, Lisa Ede, and Andrea Lunsford, among others.

My most pressing concern with Kent's "anti-process" version of post-process theory, however, is that it constructs for composition studies yet another version of its most common and most destructive binary opposition—theory versus practice. In *Constructing Knowledges,* Sidney Dobrin suggests that Kent's post-process theory "has been intruded upon by composition's pedagogical imperative" (63) in two ways: first, it has been critiqued for its lack of attention to classroom practice, and second, it has been subjected too soon to the development of pedagogical strategies. Dobrin contends that the "post-process" movement in composition studies should remain, at least for now, a purely *theoretical* enterprise, and it should consequently not yet fall victim to this pedagogical imperative (64). Yet Dobrin's desire to limit the discourse about post-process composition, first, violates the very principles of paralogy upon which this anti-process version of the post-process movement is based, and second, privileges theoretical "discourse" over pedagogical "strategies," denying that theory and pedagogy *both* construct knowledges in a dialectical process. Post-process theory, as Dobrin and Kent describe it, received its very generative impulse as a paralogic and oppositional reaction against what is arguably composition studies' most valued pedagogical strategy—teaching the composing process—yet Dobrin and Kent's post-process theory offers no pedagogical strategy of its own; regarding actual writing instruction, then, it is purely a negative dialectic.

POST-PROCESS COMPOSITION: *Extending* THE WRITING PROCESS MOVEMENT

While I argue in this chapter that the "post" in *post-process* should not represent a radical break with the composing process movement, this "post" does indeed signify *at least* a certain degree of anxiety. As I have already indicated, the writing process movement gained prominence in the college composition scene during the 1970s and retained its prominence for nearly two decades, and, according to Faigley, "it was not until the later 1980s that expressions of general disillusionment with writing as process began to be heard" (67-68). Further, John Trimbur suggests that the recent "social turn" in composition studies is the result of a "crisis within the process paradigm and a growing disillusion with its limits and pressures," and he argues that this disillusionment has generated a *"post*-process" approach to writing instruction that views "literacy as an ideological arena and composing as a cultural activity by which writers position and reposition themselves in relation to their own and others' subjectivities, discourse, practices, and institutions" (109). Those who have articulated expressions of disillusionment (though not utter despair) have critiqued the writing process movement as an expressivist and cognitivist obsession with the individual writer.

Numerous scholars, including James Berlin, Patricia Bizzell, John Clifford, Lester Faigley, and Susan Miller, among many others, argue that the individualist ideologies associated with expressivist and cognitivist approaches to composing assume a modernist conception of student writers as ultimately sovereign subjects, able to "rise above" the debilitating pressures culture and society place on the production of discourse. Yet these scholars believe that no such a-social subject exists. Instead, student writers must address rather than ignore, critique rather than dodge, the very social forces that pressure them to behave in certain institutionally advantageous ways.

It is a common perception that with this social critique of the expressivist and cognitivist writing process movement comes a necessary rejection of the composing process in general and of invention in particular, but this is simply not the case. As James Berlin, Lester Faigley, Karen Burke LeFevre, and Robert Yagelski have all pointed out, social approaches to writing instruction view composing as a process (no less than expressivist and cognitivist approaches do), yet the difference is that these approaches define composing as a social process. In *Invention as a Social Act*, for example, Karen Burke LeFevre argues that although theories of invention are commonly based on a conception of the creative individual writer, "rhetorical invention is better understood as a social act" (1). Invention methods themselves, in other words, are neither individualistic nor social; according to LeFevre, "what matters is the way the scheme is interpreted and used" (51). Thus, "the writing process," as a rubric for studying and teaching composition, is not the sole province of expressivist and cognitivist rhetorics, and the "social turn" in composition studies, which Trimbur labels "post-process," does not constitute, in practice or theory, a rejection of the process movement, but rather its extension into the social world of discourse.

Yet the problem is more complex than I have represented it so far. With the rejection of expressivist and cognitivist rhetorics from social, post-process perspectives has also come a renewed interest in "written" products, cultural "texts" from a variety of verbal and visual media. While students' own texts remain a focus in post-process composition classes, many post-process teachers believe that only using student texts in writing classes neglects fully half of the composing process, the process of *reading* cultural discourse as a form of composing. Doug Brent, for example, argues that reading is generative and forms the exigencies of future texts. M. Jimmie Killingsworth contends that new communication technologies have reintroduced "texts" into the composing process. And Louise Wetherbee Phelps urges compositionists to deconstruct the process/product opposition and reconstruct discourse structure itself as a *process*, an event, a dance. While Brent, Killingsworth, and Phelps offer very different perspectives on the issue, all agree that a renewed attention to texts in the teaching of writing enhances students' abilities to succeed in the production and reception of discourse. Whether we call them "discursive practices" (Brodkey) or "signifying practices" (Berlin, *Rhetorics, Poetics*), strategies for both reading and writing cultural texts have become a prominent focus in post-process composition classrooms.

But this renewed interest in texts by no means represents a reassertion of current-traditional ideologies into composition studies.

Whereas current-traditional writing teachers introduced *ideal* texts to their students as models, post-process writing teachers, on the other hand, introduce *cultural* texts to their students as objects of critique, as representations of social values that institutions would impose on their readers, as generative forces that comprise exigencies for writing that has meaning both inside and outside the confines of the composition class. There is little value in imitation-based *read-this-essay-and-do-what-the-author-did* pedagogical strategies, and the post-process movement in composition studies avoids this simplistic use of texts. Even so, many composition teachers who were involved in the early process versus product wars are reluctant now to acknowledge most potential uses for texts (other than those their students write) in their composition classes. While I agree that a piece of writing is "never finished," I also believe that, finished or not, most writing is read, is intended to be read, so writers must then be able to account for the ways in which texts are not only produced but also distributed and consumed within specific communities. As a means to accomplish these complicated rhetorical tasks with both the processes and products of discourse, I offer social-process rhetorical inquiry.

Social-process rhetorical inquiry, as I have described it, is a method of invention that usually manifests itself in composition classes as a set of heuristic questions based on the cycle of cultural production, contextual distribution, and critical consumption. While composition studies, I believe, has extensively explored the cognitive and social processes by which discourse is produced, the processes of distribution and consumption (and the entire cyclical process of production, distribution, and consumption) have been largely neglected. The integration of these rhetorical processes is the very function of social-process rhetorical inquiry.

Those who practice social-process rhetorical inquiry understand all communication as "discursive practice," as strategic participation in the "flow" of discourse. Discourse pre-exists the physical act of writing, and writing enters the con/texts of discourse. In order to understand how this "flow" of discourse operates, we need to engage the cycle of production, distribution, and consumption as an analytical and generative heuristic at least twice—first to *understand* how particular discursive formations operate (how their members produce, distribute, and consume discourse), and second to *enter* these discursive formations with new rhetorical interventions.

The most common "discursive formations" manifest themselves as "institutions." Norman Fairclough, in *Critical Discourse Analysis: The Critical Study of Language,* suggests that "Social actions tend very much to cluster in terms of institutions; when we witness a social event (e.g. a verbal interaction), we normally have no difficulty identifying it in institutional terms, i.e. as appertaining to the family, the school, the workplace, church, the courts, some department of government, or some other institution" (37). This is because institutions, more than any other communicative contexts, produce and structure social interactions, thereby both enabling and restricting discourse. We must, Fairclough continues, view "the institution as simultaneously facilitating and constraining the social action (here, specifically, verbal interaction) of its members: it provides them with a frame for action, without which they could not act, but it thereby constrains them to act within that frame" (38). Yet this "frame" also has much more profound consequences, for "in the process of acquiring the ways of talking which are normatively associated with [an institutionalized] subject position, one necessarily acquires also its ways of seeing, or ideological norms. And just as one is typically unaware of one's ways of talking unless for some reason they are subjected to conscious scrutiny, so also is one typically unaware of what ways of seeing, what ideological representations, underlie one's talk" (39-40). But institutions are by no means ideological monoliths: while there is often a dominant discourse promoted by high ranking members of an institution, there are also, just as often, competing discourses that vie for sub(versive)-dominance at lower levels of the hierarchy. Yet these discourses usually remain unknown or suppressed. According to Fairclough, "Naturalization gives to particular ideological representations the status of common sense, and thereby makes them opaque, i.e. no longer visible as ideologies" (42).

It is the purpose of social-process rhetorical inquiry to make visible these opaque institutional ideologies, to de-naturalize ideologies through writing, thereby helping students reconstruct perspectives on institutions that work toward more inclusive ethics. This is not to say, however, that students are completely blind to the workings of institutions. As Joseph Harris points out, most students are keenly aware of the ways in which schooling, for example, encourages certain subjectivities over others. Yet social-process rhetorical inquiry can provide for students fresh perspectives from which to observe and critique the inner workings of institutionalized socialization, enhancing the critical powers they already possess.

I prefer to focus my students' rhetorical attention through social-process rhetorical inquiry on the discourses and institutions that most profoundly impact their own lives, institutions like school, work, media, and government. In one particular assignment, my students write about the ways in which specific workplaces promote certain cultural values over others. Appendix A contains the handout students receive that guides them through the critical process of examining the cultural production, contextual distribution, and critical consumption of discourse in a workplace of their choice. It should come as no surprise that students write best about subjects that impact their lives everyday, and work has always been a generative subject for my students, whether they interrogate their own work experience or the experience of some one else in a job they would eventually like to have.

Yet I want my students to understand their (and others') work experiences in *critical, discursive,* and *institutional* ways. And in order to encourage these critical, discursive, and institutional interpretations of students' work experiences, I provide them with a complex invention heuristic that guides them through the cycle of social-process rhetorical inquiry. I have reproduced this heuristic in Appendix B. Using the invention heuristic as a guide, students generate material for their critical and practical essays. But the heuristic is only a guide and students should not feel obliged to answer all of the questions in equal depth. Some of the questions are simply not going to be relevant for every workplace and others will yield a great deal of information. For example, I have had some students write several pages of notes on "Employee Relations" and completely ignore "Geographical Layout," whereas others find that "Geographical Layout" is crucial to their understanding of various aspects of their work experience. In the pages that follow, I examine a student's response to the heuristic invention and her resulting critical and practical essay. I hope to demonstrate the important connections among the exploratory invention notes and the eventual essays, and I also hope to demonstrate the importance of encouraging students to move beyond personal narrative to institutional critique.

The following is an excerpt from Kelly Mount's invention notes on her work experience at Gapkids:

Cultural Production: Cultural values at Gapkids include: the ideal sales associate should always be at work on time, greet every customer within three minutes, offer to do anything for the customer, always sell more than one item at a time, say "thank you" and "come again," smile, answer the telephone in a cheerful voice, keep the store clean, follow the dress code.

Contextual Distribution: Methods used to reinforce the cultural values include: you have to wear Gap clothes, sales techniques are reinforced at staff meetings and in company memos, training sessions on the latest selling and display techniques. Sales are important, so we also learned how to make the store appear neat so that the clothes would be more appealing. We often worked long hours after the mall closed, cleaning and straightening the merchandise for the next day's sales.

Critical Consumption: I always followed the dress code and wore the right (Gap) clothes, greeted the customers, and tried to sell lots of items; however, I did not always feel comfortable with these requirements. What I especially hated was walking out to my car after closing. We would usually keep cleaning the store until nobody else was around. It was frightening walking to my car alone at the back of the dark parking lot.

These invention notes led Kelly to explore her experience working at Gapkids in critical ways, moving beyond her own personal experience with this workplace to an institutional critique of the cultural production, contextual distribution, and critical consumption of cultural values. Under "cultural production," Kelly explores what

Gapkids considers to be essential qualities of the ideal sales associate. These qualities/values are written from Gapkids' perspective, not Kelly's, and her goal here is simply to understand and describe Gapkids's ideal worker. Under "contextual distribution," Kelly describes specific ways in which Gapkids encourages its sales associates to strive for these ideals. Company memos, staff meetings, and employee training sessions are just a few of the "distribution" methods Gapkids uses to promote its image of the ideal sales associate. While students' notes under "cultural production" and "contextual distribution" are often brainstorming lists, their notes under "critical consumption" usually begin to acquire a center of gravity. Following her invention process, hard-sell techniques and the dangers of a dark parking lot were two ideas about which Kelly knew she would be able to write well.

Based on these invention notes, Kelly chose a few of the most important cultural values, with their attending modes of distribution and her own critique of these values and modes, and she developed them into a full critical essay. The following is one complete section of Kelly's critical essay in which she critiques the cultural value "The ideal Gapkids employee should keep the store as neat and clean as possible":

Nothing is more irritating than walking into a clothing store with a dirty floor and tables filled with unfolded, disorganized clothes. A store with this appearance does not leave a good first impression on the customer. The store seems overwhelming because you have no idea where to begin looking for a certain size or color. Shopping becomes more like a chore than a pleasurable activity. But Gapkids stores are always immaculate. When I began working at Gapkids, I was extremely surprised at how much time and effort was put into cleaning, folding clothes, and straightening the store. I recall one evening when my manager asked me to fold a stack of button-down shirts and make sure that the buttons were lined up and even. At first, I thought she was just being picky, but I soon learned that every Gapkids store expects attention paid to even the smallest details. I also remember being asked to vacuum the air vents in the ceiling one night after the store and the rest of the mall had already closed. In fact, every night after closing time, we spent an hour or two folding clothes and taking out the trash.

All of this effort put into the appearance of the store paid off economically. It created a great first impression for our customers and helped us show them the right sizes and colors without having to search the sales floor. However, all of this work did have some negative effects. Since we always had to stay for an hour or two each night after the store and mall had closed, we were usually the last people to leave the mall. This was dangerous because we were left to walk to our cars in the dark either alone or with one other worker. I think it would be better if Gapkids employees could come in an hour or two before the store opens and clean from the previous day. This would eliminate the need for sales associates to walk to their cars late at night.

Kelly structures this section of her essay into two paragraphs, each with a distinct rhetorical purpose. In the first paragraph, Kelly describes the values associated with keeping Gapkids stores neat and clean, and she does so largely from Gapkids' perspective. The ideal sales associate is, of course, charged with this important responsibility (maintaining a proper appearance) and must adopt behaviors consistent with it (vacuuming air vents, lining up buttons, etc.). Kelly plays the role in this paragraph of an advocate, describing a single value (or complex of related values) and its modes of institutional distribution, and explaining its importance in the context of Gapkids. There is no sense, yet, of critique, of evaluation, of the accommodation of worthy values, the resistance to unworthy values, or the negotiation of values that might gain some importance in alternative contexts. These are rhetorical goals that Kelly reserves for the second paragraph where she plays the role of a critic.

In her second paragraph, Kelly begins by describing and accommodating the positive aspects of the values described above (economic success, appealing to customers), and she then describes and resists some problems with these values (walking alone in a dark parking lot). Finally, Kelly negotiates a compromise (cleaning before opening rather than after closing) that retains the cultural values in question (neatness, etc.) and Gapkids's methods for promoting them (memos and meetings). In these two brief paragraphs, Kelly accomplishes a purpose that I believe has powerful significance for improving institutional discursive practices. Negotiation, the process of harnessing competing discourses (in Kelly's case, Gapkids's economic success versus employees' safety), acknowledges the importance of existing institutional values, yet it introduces other values into the mix and calls for a compromise that maintains both the established and new values. Knee jerk resistance results in oppositional audience responses and rarely accomplishes real rhetorical purposes. Ambivalent accommodation affirms the status quo. But measured negotiation enables change through compromise.

Thus far in the assignment series, Kelly has explored and critiqued the cultural production, contextual distribution, and critical consumption of institutional values promoted by Gapkids. Exploration and critique are, of course, valuable pursuits, but they should not be rhetorical ends in themselves. Through social-process rhetorical inquiry, Kelly has produced useful knowledge regarding some of the institutional practices at Gapkids; however, she has yet to use this knowledge. Thus, following this critical analysis of her work experience at Gapkids, Kelly was faced with a different rhetorical task, a more practical task, that of using her critical knowledge to write a letter that describes and solves a problem in the workplace. Kelly chose to write to the manager of the store she worked in. The following is an excerpt from that letter (which originally also addressed the problem of high-pressure sales tactics):

Kelly's Letter

Dear Ms. Doughton:

I have worked with you at Gapkids for over two years now, and I have really enjoyed my position as a sales associate. But there is something you might not be aware of that puts some of us in danger.

Several sales associates and I feel uncomfortable walking to our cars in the empty mall parking lot at 11:30 p.m. every night. I remember last week you said you were also nervous about it. I know how important it is to keep our store looking great, but there may be another way to accomplish the goal.

I've been thinking that we could schedule two employees to come in at 8:30 to clean the floors and straighten the clothes for an hour and a half before the customers arrive. This way, everybody working the night shift could leave at 10:00 p.m. when a lot of people are still around the parking lot area.

I know you have always been concerned about the welfare of your workers. Please let me know if there is anything else I can do to help you solve this problem.

Sincerely,
Kelly Mount

In this letter, Kelly is careful to acknowledge the importance of the cultural values she has observed at Gapkids (e.g., keeping the store "looking great"), yet she also introduces problems that these values cause (e.g., dangerous night-time walks in the parking lot). While much of her rhetorical efforts until this point were spent engaged in detailed exploration and critique, it is interesting to note that Kelly spends little time in her letter recounting the knowledge she generated during social-process rhetorical inquiry. Kelly knows that such critical pursuits are only appropriate in academic discourse, and the way to accomplish rhetorical goals in workplace settings is to avoid repeating information that is known or assumed and to move quickly to the point of negotiation (i.e., cleaning before the store opens). Yet we must remember that this point of negotiation arises out of the critical explorations resulting from social-process rhetorical inquiry.

Throughout this assignment series, Kelly has engaged the entire cycle of cultural production, contextual distribution, and critical consumption, first to explore and critique the cultural values promoted at Gapkids, and second to enter the flow of discourse and enable institutional change. Whether or not students actually send the letters they write is up to them; but even if the letters are not actually sent, even if they are not distributed and consumed in their target communities, students nevertheless learn valuable rhetorical strategies for future situations.

Critical writing, by means of social-process rhetorical inquiry, focuses on rhetoric, writing, and culture (all of which are inextricably intertwined) as processes, as means for accomplishing real goals both inside and outside of our classrooms. As such, it does not reject the writing process movement as a whole (though it does reject certain expressivist and cognitivist versions of it); instead, social-process rhetorical inquiry extends the writing process into the social world of discourse, the "dance" (to invoke Phelps again) of processes and products in the cycle of cultural production, contextual distribution, and critical consumption. Established process methodologies (invention strategies, revision techniques, etc.), conceived as "social acts" (LeFevre), are all key components in the cultural production of discourse. Yet social-process rhetorical inquiry extends our understanding of the composing process outward (i.e., out of the individual writer's consciousness) toward institutional processes of socialization. Writing, thus conceived, is both a way of knowing and acting, a way of understanding the world and also changing it.

NOTES

1.   It is not my goal in this section to provide a complete history of the writing process movement; instead I emphasize only a few of its aspects that are most relevant to my discussion of post-process composition.

2.   Some of the specific sources I have in mind are Peter Elbow's *Writing Without Teachers* (1973), Janet Emig's *The Composing Process of Twelfth Graders* (1971), Janice Lauer's "Heuristics and Composition" (1970), and Richard Young's "Paradigms and Problems: Much Needed Research in Rhetorical Invention" (1978).

APPENDIX A

Work Critical and Practical Essays: Assignments

In this essay, you will examine the culture of "work" critically. Most of you have either worked in the past or are currently working, and the rest of you will work in the near future. For most of us, activities associated with work will occupy about one half of our adult waking hours (8 hours of work, 8 hours of leisure, 8 hours of sleep), so it is crucial that we fully understand the cultural assumptions prevalent in our particular work situations. When we understand these cultural assumptions, we can then make informed decisions about how to live our working lives. We have the choice of accommodating, resisting, or negotiating these cultural assumptions, and in doing so we open up the potential to change the assumptions that operate against our own beliefs regarding workplace conditions and relationships.

Work Critical Essay

Those of you who have work experience (full or part-time, paid or volunteer) might write an autobiographical account of a single job you have occupied and the company that employed you. Your topic for this essay will center around a job you have (or have had) that requires you to complete a variety of tasks and interact with a number of other employees. You will derive the arguments and specific, concrete details for your work critical essay directly from your own experience in this workplace.

Those of you who have never worked might write an ethnographic description of a particular workplace and its employees. Your topic for this essay will center around a workplace to which you have easy access. You will derive the arguments and specific, concrete details for your work critical essay directly from your own detailed observations of this workplace and from interviews with its employees.

After you have decided on the general approach you would like to take in your essay (autobiographical account or ethnographic description), and you have decided on the specific workplace you would like to examine critically, then complete the invention heuristic provided for this assignment. Answer as many of the questions as you can in as much detail as you can.

After you have completed the invention heuristic, you are ready to begin writing your work critical essay. Your essay should include the following elements:

1. An introduction to the work environment and a preview of your conclusions about it. You might also include any good or bad feelings—biases—you have toward the workplace that might influence your descriptions.

2. Fully developed and well-detailed paragraphs explaining and critiquing a number of cultural values perpetuated in the workplace you are examining critically. Discuss each of these values in terms of their cultural production and contextual distribution by your employers, and your own critical consumption (accommodation, resistance, negotiation) of the values.

3. A conclusion based on ways you think the work environment might be improved.

Your audience for this critical essay should be people who have work experience in the kind of job or company you are writing about but who have not worked in exactly the same job or company. In other words, assume that your audience has fairly general knowledge of your topic but lacks specific understanding of the particular problems you have faced at work.

Work Practical Essay

Write a formal letter to someone in the workplace (a fellow worker, manager, or owner) who can do something about the problem(s) you describe in your critical essay. This letter should be approximately one single-spaced page in length, your tone in the letter should be appropriate to your audience and purpose, and you should suggest viable solutions.

Work Critical and Practical Essays: Invention Heuristic

Whether you are writing an autobiographical account of a job or an ethnographic description of a workplace, you will need to explore the topic before beginning to write. Answer the following questions in as much detail as you can. Your answers to these questions will generate details and arguments for use in your work critical essay.

Cultural Production

Use the following prompt to generate as many cultural values perpetuated in your workplace as possible: "the ideal X employee should Y." Substitute the company and job you occupy for X and the cultural effects your employers try to create in you for Y. The more cultural values you can generate, the better your selection will be when you begin writing your work critical essay.

Good cultural values are the key to a successful work critical essay. Cultural values answer the question "What kind of people do my employers want me and other employees to be?" Cultural values should be written from the perspective of the company, and they should always express qualities inherent in the ideal employee.

The following examples are well-written cultural values:

the ideal Weyerhauser factory worker is always thinking about safety first
the ideal Ray-o-Vac receptionist should always be pleasant regardless of the circumstances
the ideal Wal-Mart associate should always be busy

The following examples are poorly written cultural values:

the ideal Hardee's cook should cook each hamburger for 2:35
KinderCare preschool teachers and daycare workers should only be paid minimum wage
Nike employees think they should be promoted according to how long they have been with the company

Contextual Distribution

Brainstorm methods your employers use to reinforce (i.e., distribute) each cultural value in the workplace: job descriptions, posted policies, orientation workshops, supervision, observation, training sessions, verbal reprimands, productivity awards, staff meetings, etc. Several others should present themselves as you remember or observe your workplace.

Details regarding a company's product/service output, its employee relations and activities, and its geographical layout also contribute to the distribution of cultural values. Use the following prompts to explore how cultural values are distributed in the workplace you have chosen to critique.

Company Output: What products does the company produce and what services does it offer? What technologies are used in the company? What clientele does the company serve? Who are its target audiences? What geographical regions does the company serve?

Employee Relations: What is the power hierarchy in the company and what is your place in it? Try to draw as detailed a diagram of the company's power hierarchy as you can. What are the social relationships like among employees (workers, managers)? What kinds of interaction are allowed or encouraged among employees?

Employee Activities: What activities are assigned to your position in the company? Are your activities negotiable or strictly assigned? If negotiable, to what extent? What activities are assigned to other positions in the company? Are their activities negotiable or strictly assigned? If negotiable, to what extent?

Geographical Layout: What is the geographical layout of the company "space"? Try to draw a detailed diagram of the company's geographical layout. What "spaces" are better than others and why? Who occupies these better and worse spaces?

Critical Consumption

Describe ways that you and other employees accommodate, resist, and negotiate the cultural values perpetuated in your workplace. We accommodate work cultural values when we accept the ideal images the company places on us and we willingly complete the tasks the job requires. We resist work cultural values when we disagree with the ideal images the company places on us and we find ways to avoid or subvert the tasks the job requires. Most importantly, we negotiate work cultural values when our opinion of the ideal images the company places on us varies from situation to situation and we sometimes complete the tasks the job requires and other times avoid or subvert the same tasks.

Rhetorical Intervention

Write a letter to a member of the company that you think would be most likely (and best able) to change the workplace for the better. What members of the company are in the best position to do something about the problems you point out? List two or three as potential audiences and answer the following questions for each of them:

1. How much does the audience know about the problems you describe?
2. What is the audience's attitude toward the problems (would they want to solve them)?
3. What is your rhetorical purpose in this intervention (inform, persuade, etc.)? Choose one audience and compose a letter stating problems, describing solutions, and using an effective tone for your rhetorical purpose.

CHAPTER FOUR

Composing Postmodern Subjectivities in the Aporia between Identity and Difference

RECENT DISCUSSIONS OF TEACHING COMPOSITION IN THE CONTEXT of cultural theory have begun to consider the condition of the writing subject in society, yet these discussions often construct student-writer Subjects according to modernist identity/difference binary oppositions that are politically problematic. The modernist Subject is defined in terms of its objective relationship to reality and its opposition to "Other" subjects, and the construction of the modernist Subject (autonomous and sovereign) is an effect of ethno-centric formulations (frames, constructions) of identity/difference oppositions.[1] In *Orientalism*, for example, Edward Said describes how modernist European societies construct cultural differences not only as "other" but also as "opposite" (the identity of the West is constructed in opposition to the difference of the East). According to Said, "When one uses categories like Oriental and Western as both the starting and the end points of analysis, research, public policy, . . . the result is usually to polarize the distinction—the Oriental becomes more Oriental, the Westerner more Western—and limit the human encounter between different cultures, traditions, and societies." The tendency, then, is "to channel thought into a West or an East compartment" (46), eliminating the possibility for common ground, agreement, understanding, or in more extreme cases, destroying the human capacity for tolerance of difference. We cannot maintain oppositional notions of identity/difference without inevitably falling into a situation in which "identity" gains (or attempts to gain) hegemonic control over "difference." A few recent cultural theorists, on the other hand, do not view "identity" and "difference" as oppositional terms; instead, they construct "identity and difference" as a complementary pair, as an alliance rather than an opposition. And the subjectivities that result from this alliance refuse the structural closure of the modernist Subject and articulate themselves (engage in cultural and rhetorical practices) in the aporia between identity and difference. Michel Foucault and Jacques Derrida in particular deconstruct the unified structure of the sovereign and autonomous modernist Subject, positing in its place a space in the aporia between identity and difference where subjectivities construct themselves and each other.

Throughout much of his work, Foucault is concerned with issues of identity and difference in the textual construction of subjectivities. Discursive formations (networks of language, terministic screens that condition perception and organize power relations) normalize human agents, presenting to them modes of discourse that do not threaten the status quo and concealing from them potentially liberatory modes of discourse. One's identity is constructed through the language of a given discursive formation, and it is strengthened in its differentiation (the illegitimate, often evil difference) from other human agents normalized differently by other discursive formations. In *The Order of Things*, for example, Foucault argues that "Resemblance, which had for long been the fundamental category of knowledge—both the form and the content of what we know—became dissociated in an analysis based on terms of *identity* and *difference*" (my emphasis, 54). Within this ordering framework of identity and difference, Foucault continues, the

> activity of the mind . . . will therefore no longer consist in drawing things together, in setting out on a quest for everything that might reveal some sort of kinship, attraction, or secretly shared nature within them, but, on the contrary, in discriminating, that is, in establishing their identities,

then the inevitability of the connections with all the successive degrees of a series. In this sense, discrimination imposes upon comparison the primary and fundamental investigation of difference: providing oneself by intuition with a distinct representation of things, and apprehending clearly the inevitable connection between one element in a series and that which immediately follows it. (55)

Conceptions of thought and order as products of identity/difference oppositions form the central problematic in the constitution of the modernist Subject, and Foucault's institutional genealogies interrogate these processes of Subject formation (Subjectification). Discursive formations—institutionalized dominant discourses regarding punishment, sexuality, madness, etc.—construct and socialize Subjects; discursive formations give the illusion that they represent the Truth of the world and that this objective Truth may be known by any sovereign Subject who chooses to pursue it. But the effectiveness of the modernist discursive formation in constructing loyal Subjects through the illusion of sovereignty, through the illumination of identity and difference, is problematized by the critical practice of genealogy, a methodology Foucault uses to lay bare the oppressive forces at work in various discursive formations' constructions of identity/difference oppositions.

Like Foucault, Derrida also objects to the closure of the modernist metaphysical Subject and the structural autonomy of the sovereign self that does not account for trace and *différance*; instead, Derrida argues, we should discover our own subjectivities and identities in the very difference and alterity that once constituted the modernist "Other," thus destroying in the process the oppositional character of identity and difference and opening a space—an aporia—between them for postmodern cultural and rhetorical practices. In *The Other Heading*, his attempt to account for the collapse of Eastern European Communism and the political fragmentation in Europe generally, Derrida deconstructs the identity/difference opposition which, he argues, leads inevitably to physical and metaphysical violence: "Hope, fear, and trembling are commensurate with the signs that are coming to us from everywhere in Europe, where,

precisely in the name of identity, be it cultural or not, the worst vio-
lences, . . . the crimes of xenophobia, racism, anti-Semitism, religious
or nationalist fanaticism, are being unleashed" (my emphasis, 6).
Modernist Subject-identity is constructed, according to Derrida,
through the gathering of differences—an affinity of differences—to
others; we construct ourselves according to what we perceive in others that we do not perceive in ourselves—the repulsive, the strange,
the particular that does not participate in the universal, as we
our(modernist)Selves do.

> Whether it takes a national form or not, a refined, hospitable or aggres-
> sively xenophobic form or not, the self-affirmation of an identity always
> claims to be responding to the call or assignation of the universal. . . . No
> cultural identity presents itself as the opaque body of an untranslatable
> idiom, but always, on the contrary, as the irreplaceable *inscription* of the
> universal in the singular, the *unique testimony* to the human essence and
> to what is proper to man. (72-73)

In place of this Enlightenment conception of the Subject that
leads inevitably to violence, Derrida presents an "axiom" that he
believes should guide our postmodern conception of subjectivity:
"what is proper to a culture [or subjectivity] is not to be identical to
itself" (9). Derrida explains that this does not mean "not to have an
identity, but not to be able to identify itself, to be able to say 'me' or
'we'; to be able to take the form of a subject only in the non-identity
to itself or, if you prefer, only in the difference with itself" (9-10). In
postmodern notions of identity, then, "there is no self-relation, no
relation to oneself, no identification with oneself, without culture,
but a culture of oneself *as* a culture *of* the other, a culture . . . of the
difference to oneself " (10). The problem, according to Derrida, is that
modernist cultures and Enlightenment Subjects understand themselves as "headings," as leaders of other cultures and other Subjects,
and Derrida applies this modernist conception of the Enlightenment
Nation/Subject to the recent troubles in Eastern Europe:

> Europe is not only a geographical headland or heading that has always
> given itself the representation or figure of a spiritual heading, at once as

project, task, or infinite—that is to say universal—idea, as the memory of itself that gathers and accumulates itself, capitalizes upon itself, in and for itself. Europe has also confused its image, its face, its figure and its very place, its taking-place, with that of an advanced point, the point of a phallus if you will, and thus, once again, with a heading for world civilization or human culture in general. The idea of an advanced point of *exemplarity* is the *idea of the* European *idea*, its *eidos*, at once as *arch*é—the idea of beginning but also of commanding (the *cap* as the head, the place of capitalizing memory and of decision, once again, the captain)—and as *telos*, the idea of the end, of a limit that accomplishes, or that puts an end to the whole point of the achievement, right there at the point of completion. The advanced point is at once beginning and end, it is divided as beginning and end; it is the place from which or in view of which everything takes place. (24-25)

Later in *The Other Heading*, Derrida presents a paradox which he believes points toward an answer to the problems facing Europe in the final decade of the twentieth century: *"on the one hand,"* Derrida argues,

> European cultural identity . . . cannot and must not be dispersed into a myriad of provinces, into a multiplicity of self-enclosed idioms or petty little nationalisms, each one jealous and untranslatable. . . . But, *on the other hand,* it cannot and must not accept the capital of a centralizing authority that, by means of trans-European cultural mechanisms, by means of publishing, journalistic, and academic concentrations—be they state-run or not—would control and standardize, subjecting artistic discourses and practices to a grid of intelligibility, to philosophical or aesthetic norms, to channels of immediate and efficient communication, to the pursuit of ratings and commercial profitability. (38-39)

This same paradox may be applied to postmodern subjectivities in the aporia between identity and difference: postmodern subjectivities must not disperse into a politically impotent multiplicity of different individuals, and they must not accept centralizing authorities that coagulate differences into politically impotent universalizing identities.

Modernist thought, according to Derrida, frames this identity/difference paradox as an unresolvable contradiction; however, postmodern thought views the paradox as having an aporia, a middle territory that can be articulated rhetorically: "Responsibility seems to consist today in renouncing neither of these two contradictory imperatives. One must therefore try to invent gestures, discourses, politico-institutional practices that inscribe the alliance of these two imperatives" (44). We should begin, in other words, to abandon our alliance with an illusion of the universal, and we must merge the concerns of our own "heading" with the concerns of the "headings" of others; we should begin to establish our own heading in accordance with the heading of the other without abandoning our own heading or rejecting the heading of the other; we should open our own heading to the heading of the other. This paradoxical practice, this opening of the heading to the other, this postmodern formation of identity in alliance with difference (rather than in modernist opposition to it) implies a number of duties: "welcoming foreigners in order not only to integrate them but to recognize and accept their alterity"; "criticizing a religion of capital that institutes its dogmatism under new guises," and "cultivating the virtue of such critique, of the critical idea, the critical tradition, but also submitting it, beyond critique and questioning, to a deconstructive genealogy that thinks and exceeds it without yet compromising it" (77); assuming "an idea of democracy" that is "never simply given" and "remains to be thought"; "respecting differences, idioms, minorities, singularities, but also the . . . desire for translation, agreement and univocity, the law of the majority, opposition to racism, nationalism, and xenophobia" (78); "respecting all that is not placed under the authority of reason," such as faith (78-79). We all have the duty, the responsibility to "think, speak, and act in compliance with this double contradictory imperative" (79). Through these practices, Derrida argues, we can articulate postmodern subjectivities that are not mutually exclusive, and we can live in a postmodern world without being paralyzed by the violence of warring factions.

IDENTITY AND DIFFERENCE IN THE CLASSROOM

These Foucauldian and Derridean deconstructions of modernist Subjects as products of identity/difference oppositions problematize much of the cultural theory frequently drawn upon in social composition pedagogies. The rhetorical us/them violence that, according to Derrida, has led to real violence in Eastern Europe ought not to be encouraged in courses directed toward developing critical social consciousness in our composition students. When we teach students to read cultural texts through binary terministic screens, we only limit their abilities to negotiate these texts. One goal of my own composition pedagogy is to encourage in students a certain cultural initiative in their understanding and use of the texts I assign in class, a cultural initiative that is diminished by binary politics. But the difficult question is a pedagogical one: How can we *teach* students to avoid the binary logic of identity/difference oppositions in their critical writing about culture?

During the first three weeks of many of the composition courses I teach, my students focus on what I call "position statements." These position statements introduce students to the active reading strategies they will need in the rest of the course. When we ask students to read and write about culture, they tend to think in binary logics: students often view the cultural artifacts I bring to class and the social institutions we discuss each week as being either right or wrong, good or bad; and their responses to articles having to do with these artifacts and institutions can usually be summarized "I agree/disagree with the author(s)." This binary perspective through which students approach cultural artifacts and social institutions is attributable, I believe, to their perception of themselves and the authors of assigned texts as modernist Subjects. When students construct themselves through identity/difference oppositions, the only choices they have to make in approaching a cultural artifact or critiquing a social institution will be: Is it like me, and does it possess identities to myself? Or is it not like me, and does it possess differences from myself? But it is my goal to help students move beyond identity/difference oppositions that only encourage accommodation or resistance; it is my goal to help them *negotiate* cultural artifacts, social institutions, and articles about these artifacts and institutions in postmodern ways. Negotiation, however, requires that students learn active reading strategies that most are simply unfamiliar with when they enter college.

During the first week of classes, I describe the position statement assignment to students using the following paragraphs as a guide:

> Throughout this course, you will write several "position statements"— short writing experiences designed to help you develop active reading strategies—in response to assigned texts that argue competing sides of a cultural issue. Each position statement requires you to critique the assigned articles from your own perspective, *accommodating* and acknowledging good ideas (and explaining why they are good), *resisting* and rejecting bad ideas (and explaining why they are bad), and—most importantly—*negotiating* and revising ideas (and explaining how they might best be revised), *referring always to your own cultural experiences.*
>
> Accommodation and resistance in position statements only require us to state our agreement or disagreement with the ideas that are already present in the assigned texts. But negotiation, a far more valuable critical reading strategy, requires us to establish our own position in the middle ground among competing texts. In other words, when we negotiate assigned texts, we articulate the points of intersection among both the texts themselves and our own cultural experiences. In order to discover these points of intersection, though, we must do more than simply read to ascertain the content of the assigned essays; we must read instead to understand their lives as texts—their spirit, their politics, their history, their investments—and how their lives as texts intersect with our own lives as readers.

The instructions are vague and intentionally so, until we move into our first context for critical reading and writing.

Our first context centers on rap music, in particular the banning of 2 Live Crew's album *As Nasty as They Wanna Be* by Judge Jose Gonzalez in a federal district court in Ft. Lauderdale, Florida. Students are asked to write a position statement on two essays that represent competing views of the 2 Live Crew controversy: "Rap: Slick, Violent, Nasty, and, Maybe, Hopeful" by Jon Pareles (originally published in the *New York Times* on June 17, 1990) and "America's Slide into the Sewer" by George Will (originally published in *Newsweek* on July 30, 1990).[2] Briefly, Pareles admits that 2 Live Crew's rap lyrics represent violence, but he vindicates slick and nasty rappers for their political integrity and their subcultural battle against dominant culture's racist stereotypes. Will, on the other hand, condemns rap lyrics, particularly those in 2 Live Crew's banned album, for directly inciting African-American youth to sexually violent behavior.

The following excerpts from three students' position statements demonstrate the spirit of negotiation and the formation of subject positions in the aporia between identity-with and difference-from the arguments advanced by both Pareles and Will. Kristina Dickerson, an African American woman though not a member of the urban culture that generates rap music, negotiates a subject position with a broader knowledge-base than Pareles and Will demonstrate, and the alternative subject position she constructs in the aporia between Pareles and Will leads her to a favorable opinion of rap in general:

> In my own experience, rappers such as Queen Latifah demand respect for women and also teach women to command respect for themselves. Other rappers such as De La Soul praise peace above violence, and many other groups rap about drug use and its downfalls. These artists' songs should not be censored. If everyone listened to all kinds of rap instead of just the hard-core, violence filled rap that makes the headlines, they would find a very rich culture with an important message being sent to the youth of America.

Kristina views the banning of 2 Live Crew's *As Nasty as They Wanna Be* as a symptom of synecdochal generalization: she does not approve of the lyrics in some rap music—particularly 2 Live Crew's—but she more strongly opposes condemning the entire musical genre, which often contains positive messages about race, gender, and class relations, because of a few grandstanders. For her, even though 2 Live Crew is wrong to rap the way they do, to ban one of their albums is to brand all rap music "obscene," which quite simply is not the case. Kristina accepts Will's conclusion that the violent and degrading rap lyrics in 2 Live Crew's banned album may encourage self-destructive behavior among African-American youth, yet she rejects Will's conservative impulse to synecdochally generalize his particular conclusion regarding one rap group to all the rest.

Kristina also accepts Pareles' desire to vindicate 2 Live Crew for their subcultural opposition to dominant culture; however, she is not inclined, as Pareles is, to overlook the violence and degradation represented in their lyrics. Instead, Kristina invokes the socially conscientious lyrics of rappers like Queen Latifah and De La Soul who write about violence and degradation as negative forces in African-American communities; and through her invocation of these alternative rap groups and their socially constructive lyrics, Kristina is able to forge her own complex subject position in the aporia between "liberal" Pareles and "conservative" Will.

Sheri North has little personal experience listening to rap music, so she negotiates a subject position in the aporia between Pareles and Will by referring to the Christian music she likes and what it means to her; and in making this comparison, Sheri constructs rap as an important cultural symbol which should be protected:

> Rap has become a cultural symbol concerned with the experiences and lives of African-American communities. Likewise, Christian music serves as a cultural symbol for my family because it deals with the experiences of everyday Christians and how we should live our lives and put all our trust in God. . . . Vulnerable individuals who listen to rap may think that the violent lyrics describe the right way of doing things. However, sometimes rap does serve as a creative channel for expressing alienation and oppression.

Sheri's reading of Pareles and Will is conflicted: she believes that rap music is vulgar and violent (as does Will), and she disapproves of it on that basis. Yet Sheri also sees rap as a cultural symbol of African-American social history (as does Pareles), much like gospel music and hymns are cultural symbols of her own Christian social history. In terms of censorship, rap's character as a cultural symbol overpowers its character as a representation of violence and degradation, but the symbolic character of rap music in no way excuses the crude content of its lyrics. From Sheri's Christian subject position, rap music is a social bane. However, Sheri is able to recognize and accept the differences between her own community's values and the values of urban African-American communities that generate rap music; and Sheri embraces these differences, gathering them together in an alliance based on cultural symbolism.

Like Sheri, Jodi Warden does not listen to rap music; however, she does work in a daycare center, and she sees first-hand the influences media have on children's actions. Jodi formulates a subject position in the aporia between Pareles and Will based on her own experience with groups of children—experience that neither Pareles nor Will presumably share—and she criticizes rap on the basis of her interactions with these children:

> 2 Live Crew may not be out doing what they sing about, but their music seems to make people, especially kids, want to. Rap is not a productive outlet. It is obvious to me that the things kids listen to and watch on TV have a profound effect on their actions. For example, the new cartoon show *Power Rangers* deals with a group of kids who fight and kill bad people. A number of daycare centers, including the one I work at, have banned children from watching this show because the children act out the fighting on the playground. Children act out what they see, and it is logical to assume they would do the same with what they hear.

Jodi condemns rap music for its complicity in a larger social problem—the negative effects media have on children's behavior—and she opposes Pareles on principled grounds. Jodi's experience as a daycare worker allows her to understand in concrete ways the social problems to which violent media (one of which is rap) contribute. However, Jodi's forceful rejection of Pareles' liberal arguments regarding the rap music controversy does not cause her to accept impulsively Will's conservative arguments; she does not, in other words, fall backwards into the prefabricated subject position Will provides in his article. Instead, Jodi draws on her own extensive experience with children and forms in the process her own subject position. Whereas Kristina and Sheri construct subject positions in the "middle" (if you will) of the aporia between Pareles and Will, Jodi's subject position tends to slant more in the direction of Will. Jodi does not, however, accommodate uncritically the arguments Will presents; instead, she formulates an alternative subject position, different from Will's, from which to approach the rap music controversy and the banning of *As Nasty as*

They Wanna Be. Jodi recognizes definite affinities between her own position and Will's, yet she looks to her experience with children to find differences and to construct them in a conservative alliance against what she perceives as a social ill.

In their position statements, Kristina, Sheri, and Jodi critique the competing ideas presented in the articles by Pareles and Will, but their critiques are rooted solidly in their own cultural experience. These three students, in other words, do not passively accommodate or defensively resist the arguments advanced by Pareles or Will; and they avoid, consequently, falling easily into prefabricated liberal and conservative subject positions. Instead, these students negotiate the texts through the filters of their own terministic screens, constructing alternative subject positions in the aporia between identity-to and difference-from Pareles and Will. Kristina, Sheri, and Jodi gather the arguments advanced in the articles by Pareles and Will into an alliance of differences, and the force that gathers them together is the personal experience each author is able to bring to the rhetorical situation. In position statement assignments, students are "thrown" into a multiplicity of competing discourses and asked to derive meaning of their own through them; they are asked to articulate, without falling into either/or logic, a subject position among the points of divergence constructed in cultural texts.

Position statements help students approach texts with critical eyes and with the intent to construct their own subject positions rather than passively accommodating or defensively resisting those offered to them (and authored for them) in a variety of media. Position statements teach students the active reading strategies necessary for writing effective cultural studies essays on the semiotic significance of their own experiences (and others' experiences represented in outside texts, both assigned in class and acquired through research) in work, advertising, and school contexts. I have found that students are better prepared for more involved cultural studies writing assignments once they have had experience finding and articulating subject positions in the aporia between identity and difference within a number of cultural contexts.

As I have already explained, most of the cultural studies writing assignments that I design have two parts: a critical essay in which students describe and critique competing discourses in an institutional context, and a practical document in which students attempt to gather the differences among competing discourses into an alliance and propose resolutions to one of the problems described in their critical essays. Too often we find social composition pedagogies neglecting the rhetorical function of critical knowledge; these practical documents teach students how effectively to use the knowledge they gain through critique. For example, one of the first full-length essays students write in my cultural studies composition classes examines "work" as a critical context. In these essays, students locate the competing discourses in a current or former place of employment (those who have no work experience write ethnographic essays) and compose critical essays that formulate subject positions in the aporia between or among the competing discourses at the workplace. The students' next task is to write a practical document that attempts to reconcile the competing discourses and resolve a problem associated with them. In these practical documents, students draw forcefully on the active reading strategies they learned in their earlier position statements: practical documents must not represent one ideological pole of the competing discourses in the work context under examination; they must instead reconcile these competing discourses, gathering their differences together into an alliance of differences directed at a common goal—the improvement of the work environment for all employees.

Kim Yates, for example, a student in one of my cultural studies composition classes, wrote her work-critical essay on Champagne Dye Works in North Carolina, a factory in her hometown. The competing discourses Kim locates in her critical essay center around social and economic class distinctions and physical working conditions. During the time Kim was employed at Champagne Dye Works, she had not graduated from high school and was in no position to pick and choose among employment opportunities. She took the first offer made to her, as did most of her uneducated (though older) colleagues working in the dye works factory. Material working conditions at Champagne Dye Works were difficult to endure for factory workers—no air conditioning in the summer and no heat in the winter caused health problems for many employees—but management offices were equipped with the necessary environmental control technologies. In her critical essay, Kim prints part of an interview that represents the discourse of uneducated factory workers at Champagne Dye Works. In this interview, Peggy Green explains her predicament: "With me being fifty-three with no education, I feel it would be really hard for me to find another job, and it is too late for me to go back to school." The uneducated workers at Champagne Dye Works were in no position to complain about the poor working conditions they endured each day, since management could quite easily "find another body to replace you." Kim also represents the discourse of the management at Champagne Dye Works, though only indirectly, acknowledging that the expense of fully heating and air conditioning the entire factory would be overwhelming.

The practical letter Kim wrote to the owner of Champagne Dye Works reconciles the competing discourses into an alliance of differences, and she harnesses these differences in the service of a common goal: to improve worker morale without excessive cost. Kim suggests that the owner of Champagne Dye Works set specific "control temperatures" above and below which workers would be encouraged to take frequent alternating breaks in limited and environmentally controlled spaces to rest and recover from adverse conditions. Through these critical and practical essays, Kim recognized that adopting only one of the competing subject positions within the context of Champagne Dye Works (i.e., uneducated worker vs. privileged management) would be rhetorically ineffective; in order potentially to enact change in the material conditions of uneducated workers, Kim had to gather into alliance the differences between uneducated workers and privileged management and enlist those differences toward a common goal. While Kim does not directly confront privileged management with their unethical social treatment of working class individuals, the rhetorical tone of her letter to the owner of

Champagne Dye Works does propose implicitly a more inclusive ethic in their treatment of uneducated workers. Kim demonstrates, through her writings in the context of work, the kind of complicated thought that is characteristic of effective cultural criticism and that can potentially lead to social change.

Students in composition courses that focus on cultural categories (race, class, gender), popular artifacts (television, advertising, pulp fiction), and/or institutions (work, school, religion) benefit from rhetorical and cultural strategies that teach them to avoid the paralyzing either/or logic of identity/difference binary oppositions. For example, students who can construct subject positions in the aporia among competing discourses are equipped to offer viable cultural alternatives to the processes that marginalize certain people. These students work to negotiate cultural identities and differences, representing the unrepresented and re-representing those represented in marginalizing ways. This socio-rhetorical strategy of negotiation is learned initially through writing position statements and developed through composing critical and practical essays in a variety of cultural contexts. This, I urge, must be the goal of cultural studies composition courses: to teach students to change the cultures that affect them everyday by deconstructing binary representations while constructing culturally humane and rhetorically effective subject positions in the aporia between identity and difference.

NOTES

1. The oppressive character of the modernist Subject has been rehearsed by a number of scholars in composition studies; for the most complete treatments, see John Clifford's "The Subject in Discourse," Diana George and Diane Shoos's "Issues of Subjectivity and Resistance," and Susan Miller's *Rescuing the Subject* and *Textual Carnivals*.

2. These two articles are anthologized in the textbook I required for the class: Diana George and John Trimbur's *Reading Culture: Contexts for Critical Reading and Writing;* they do not appear in the 2nd (1995) or 3rd (1999) editions.

CHAPTER FIVE

Critical Discourse Analysis in the Composition Class

COMPOSITION TEACHERS OFTEN FORAGE IN LINGUISTICS FOR NEW ways to approach issues of style, grammar, and invention in their classrooms; however, in "Linguistics and Composition Instruction, 1950-1980," Sharon Crowley points out that since traditional linguistics views language as acontextual and has little concern for discourse beyond sentence length, the value of linguistics for composition studies is limited. While Crowley's conclusions are consistent with the state of linguistics from the 1950s through the 1960s, there were, as Frank Parker and Kim Sydow Campbell suggest, important developments in linguistics shortly before 1970 and thereafter. One development in particular (not pursued by Parker and Campbell) is the overtly "rhetorical" systemic and functional linguistics articulated by M. A. K. Halliday, as well as other linguistic theories that claim Halliday as their foundation.[1] During the late 1960s and 1970s, Halliday was developing his functional linguistic theories in such works as *Grammar, Society and the Noun, Explorations in the Functions of Language, Learning How to Mean,* and *System and Function in Language,* arguing throughout these works that language structure is a function of language use, and language use is a function of social context. Meanwhile, a group of linguists at the University of East Anglia, Roger Fowler, Gunther Kress, Robert Hodge, and Tony Trew, were paying close attention. These four linguists began to merge Halliday's rhetorical (functional, systemic) linguistic methodologies with critical theories of culture and ideology, and in *Language and Control*, published in 1979, they formally called their resulting hybrid "Critical Linguistics" (CL). More recently, Critical Discourse Analysis (CDA), a branch of CL, has extended its objects of inquiry beyond just the structure of texts (CL's obsession) toward the processes of discursive production and interpretation (Fairclough, *Language* 22-27), drawing its inspiration not only from functional and systemic linguistics but also from a variety of leftist and Marxist cultural critics, including Antonio Gramsci, Louis Althusser, Mikhail Bakhtin, Michel Foucault and Jurgen Habermas (Fairclough and Wodak 260-62). In this chapter, I argue that these recent developments in linguistics, particularly in the area of CDA—developments thus far largely neglected in composition studies—have much to contribute to social methods for the teaching of writing.

CDA is the politically committed practice of text linguistics, and when applied to composition studies through social-process rhetorical inquiry, CDA encourages in students an attention to language as the perceptible embodiment of otherwise illusive ideologies and power relations. While many in composition studies have articulated thoughtful and detailed pedagogies based on important social theory, these pedagogies often lack a textual focus that we can gain through the incorporation of CDA into our classes. Recent edited collections such as *Left Margins, Reclaiming Pedagogy, Composition and Resistance, Social Issues in the English Classroom, Pedagogy in the Age of Politics,* and *Miss Grundy Doesn't Teach Here Anymore,* for example, do much to advance our awareness of how to teach writing and texts as social and cultural phenomena, yet the pedagogies contained in these collections tend to focus more on the content rather than the language of reading and writing assignments; they focus more on the idea of socialization than on the linguistic and semiotic means by which socialization is accomplished. But CDA, when taught in conjunction with other kinds of social writing pedagogies, offers teachers and students a more systematic method for studying the language of cultural texts—the means by which socialization and subject positioning occur—than most current social approaches to teaching writing offer.

In order to explore CDA's uses in the teaching of writing, I begin this chapter with a description of the relevance of CDA to composition studies; second, I describe two writing assignments and a social-process invention heuristic based on CDA; and third, I discuss specific pedagogical methods for teaching these assignments and heuristic.

CRITICAL DISCOURSE ANALYSIS AND COMPOSITION STUDIES

Unlike traditional linguists, practitioners of CDA turn their analytical and critical tools not only toward the structure of language itself but also toward the cultural contexts surrounding language use, the social relations of communicators, and the modes (oral, written, visual) of semiotic interaction. But more than this theoretical focus, what unites CDA practitioners is their political commitment to subverting social and cultural oppression. As Kress explains, CDA "has from the beginning had a political project: . . . to bring a system of excessive inequalities into crisis by uncovering its workings and its effects through the analysis of potent cultural objects—texts—and thereby to help in achieving a more equitable social order" ("Representational" 15). Active and passive constructions, for example, are not simply value-free variant transformations of the same kernel sentence; from a CDA perspective, they are political choices that either acknowledge or efface certain human agents in a social dialogue—they are concrete manifestations of ideological work. CDA practitioners examine the political effects that such linguistic constructions as passivation, nominalization, classification, and generalization (among many others) have on the representation of subjectivities.

While innovative and useful, CDA, in its earliest manifestations, was problematic in at least two respects. Kay Richardson and Lester Faigley, for example, have both noted that the earliest approaches to CDA, despite overt claims to the contrary, still privileged text over context and assumed a simplistic base/superstructure model of ideology. Faigley argues, "Linguistic theory that attempts to relate language to social practice can offer ways to begin discussing the unstated cultural assumptions of texts, but linguistic analyses . . . are incomplete unless they take into account the specific historical circumstances in which these texts were produced and read" (97-98). More recent CDA practitioners, however, including Teun van Dijk and Norman Fairclough, have worked to resolve the problems that plagued their predecessors, and even some of the original East Anglia critical linguists, Hodge and Kress in particular, have embraced the different directions in which CDA has gone during the past several years.[2] In this newer model of CDA, Critical Linguistics still provides methods for text analysis; however, since, as Fairclough points out in *Language and Power*, the term *discourse* refers to "the whole process of social interaction of which a text is just a part" (24), current CDA practitioners also consider the processes of production, distribution, and consumption within which texts are generated and circulated.

During the 1980s and 1990s, the work of CDA has been taken up by socially committed linguists interested in critiquing institutional contexts as much as the texts produced within them. For example, van Dijk's most recent scholarship (including *Elite Discourse and Racism* and *Racism and the Press*) examines the discursive construction of ethnic differences in particular institutional contexts. Further, as founding and current editor of *Discourse & Society*, the first and still most prominent site for CDA scholarship, van Dijk has provided a much needed forum for emerging scholars interested in extending CDA into the realm of institutional critique. Fairclough, perhaps CDA's best known proponent, has focused much of his energy on theorizing this still-emerging and complex discipline. In *Discourse and Social Change*, for example, Fairclough views discourse itself as a social practice, and he locates CDA at the intersection of Marxist cultural studies, poststructuralist discourse theories, and critical linguistics methodologies, suggesting that it is in the convergence of these that CDA gains its explanatory and political power.

In order for CDA to enact real change in the social order, it must, according to Kress, "be able to move from critical reading, from analysis, from deconstructive activity, to productive activity"

("Representational" 15-16); the critical task of CDA, in other words, "must be turned around to become an enterprise focused on *making*" (19). And there is simply no better site in which to emphasize the making of discourse than the composition class. I argue that the best way students can implement the principles of CDA in their writing classes is through the following four-fold methodology: first, through *analyzing* the cultural and social values encoded into a target discourse; second, through *identifying* potential alternative cultural and social values disguised by certain linguistic and rhetorical choices in the target discourse; third, through *critiquing* the cultural and social values encoded into the target discourse from the perspective of potential alternative discourses; and fourth, through producing new discourses that encode alternative cultural and social values for the purpose of intervening in certain institutional processes of socialization.

Writing assignments that require extensive preparation, provoke thoughtful critical reading, and elicit the production of discursive interventions, in my own experience, encourage fully developed and vigorously argued essays. Students who complete these assignments do not enter the classroom as blank slates (the "duped masses") or as individuals automatically predisposed to exercise critique rather than feel pleasure. Instead, as both Joseph Harris and Frank Farmer suggest, these students are encouraged to extend the critical powers that they already possess, developing them even further through guided heuristic inquiry. Social-process heuristics foster a dialogic interaction between writers and the objects of their critiques, an interaction that results most often in a balance of accommodation, resistance, and negotiation. In the next section of this chapter, I describe two writing assignments and a CDA-based social-process heuristic for rhetorical inquiry into the semiotics of college viewbooks.

CRITIQUING AND PRODUCING CULTURAL AND SOCIAL VALUES IN COLLEGE VIEWBOOKS

Before I detail each individual section of the viewbook assignments and heuristic, let me first provide an impression of the whole.

The entire viewbook project has two major parts. Assignment one, "Critiquing Cultural and Social Values in College Viewbooks," focuses on critical writing, and its goal is to help students develop "representational resources," as Kress calls them, i.e., learned sets of textual characteristics that students have seen other communicators use. Here students complete detailed invention notes in response to a CDA-based social-process heuristic for rhetorical inquiry into the social semiotics of college viewbooks, and they write critical essays explaining and critiquing the cultural and social values promoted in the viewbooks. Assignment two, "Producing Cultural and Social Values in College Viewbooks," focuses on pragmatic writing, composing for specific audiences with the aim of influencing their actions and beliefs, and the goal of assignment two is to help students develop "representational processes," i.e., learned strategies for composing and methods for achieving desired textual characteristics. Here students generate detailed lists of the cultural and social values that they want to promote for the school they currently attend, and they write a viewbook of their own, using rhetorical strategies (both verbal and visual) that work to promote those values.

Although there are myriad choices of discourses for students to critique and produce in this kind of writing assignment, I choose college viewbooks for two specific reasons. First, the viewbooks themselves represent *institutional* discourse more clearly than other kinds of texts. Before they even open a viewbook, most students have some knowledge of what to expect; students understand that the values of a religious college will be different from the values of a secular college, and these kinds of institutional expectations invite exploration. Since most college viewbooks can be categorized as "advertising" kinds of texts (their audience is undecided prospective students, and their aim is to persuade these students to enroll), viewbooks are more overt about the values they promote than other institutional discourses that do not have an advertising function. And values are political. College viewbooks, as institutional discourses, function to promote their values by encouraging certain kinds of students to enroll and discouraging other kinds of students. Second, writing students are most interested in subjects that profoundly affect their lives, and college students, especially freshmen, benefit from this viewbook assignment because, more than any other students, they are actively involved in the process of discovering their own identities in relation to the new academic cultures that surround them.

The following handout describes assignment one of the viewbook project:

Assignment One
Critiquing Cultural and Social Values in College Viewbooks

For this assignment, you will critique the representations of cultural values, social values, and their associated ideal identities constructed in a viewbook from a specific type of college or university (hereafter I will just use "college" to refer to all post-secondary schools). You may choose the viewbook that most interests you from the following list of college types:

Women's Colleges	Men's/Coed Colleges
Technical or Trade Colleges	Liberal Arts Colleges
Private: Selective Colleges	Public: Open Admissions Colleges
2 Year Colleges	4 Year Colleges
Religious Colleges	Secular Colleges

First, analyze and critique the cultural values represented in the viewbook and the ideal student identities associated with them. Second, analyze and critique the social values represented in the college viewbook and the ideal social citizen identities associated with them.

This first assignment introduces students to certain key terms that require definitions and discussion. First, "cultural values" describe characteristics of the ideal community inside the college itself, and within the context of the ideal college community there must be ideal students (or ideal student identities) to lead the community to its utopian goal. Each kind of college promotes different cultural values and attracts, accordingly, different student identities, and these values and identities are foregrounded in their respective viewbooks. Yet colleges and students are only "ideal" from certain perspectives, and often viewbooks' representations of model colleges and students have their foundations in elitist, ethnocentric, and sexist assumptions. Students should learn, then, to read these media more critically than they already do, accommodating "good" cultural values and student identities (inclusive, sensitive to economic, social, and political difference), resisting "bad" cultural values and student identities (exclusive, exploitative of economic, social, and political difference), and negotiating the cultural values and student identities whose worth must be determined by context. Students must determine for themselves, however, based on their own criteria, which values and identities they should accommodate, resist, and negotiate.

Next, "social values" describe characteristics of an ideal society outside the context of the college in question. Since the function of education is to prepare future social citizens, it is crucial that students understand how the world outside the college is represented in the context of the viewbook. Social values describe characteristics of an ideal society, and there must be ideal social citizens (or ideal college graduates) to lead this society to its utopian goal. Each kind of college promotes different social values and attracts, accordingly, students with different future social citizen identities, and these values and identities are foregrounded in their respective viewbooks. Yet societies and their social citizens are only "ideal" from certain perspectives, and when students examine them from potential alternative perspectives these "ideals" often break down.

Having carefully defined the key terms and explored students' tasks in the first assignment, we then proceed to the invention handout, which I present to students in four sections. The first two sections focus on the cultural values and student identities within the college context, and the third and fourth sections focus on the social values and ideal social citizen identities in a broader context outside the college itself. Perhaps the most important thing for students to remember during their social-process rhetorical inquiries is that not all four sections of the heuristic will be equally useful for all view-books. Some viewbooks, for example, focus mostly on establishing cultural values for their college communities, while others focus more on establishing social values. Students should at least attempt thoughtful responses to every prompt in the four-part heuristic, but they should also feel free to focus their inquiries in the areas of the heuristic that most effectively facilitate the critique of the viewbook in question. The purpose of the heuristic is to guide students toward sharpening their critical knowledge of both the cultural and social values (with their attending ideal identities) encoded in the view-book, yet most students' resulting critical essays focus mostly on information generated from just one, two, or sometimes three of the heuristic's four sections.

First, students explore how their viewbook produces certain cultural values, and they critique these values from potential alternative perspectives. The heuristic for this first critical operation follows:

Cultural Values Inside the College

Analyze the viewbook's description of cultural values (brainstorm):

- List the key words/phrases in the viewbook that describe college culture.
- Transcribe verbal passages in the viewbook that describe college culture.
- Describe the predominant visual images in the viewbook that depict college culture.
- List the cultural values that these words/phrases, passages, and images imply. (The ideal college should . . .)

Identify alternative cultural values not described in the viewbook (brainstorm):

- List different or opposing key words/phrases that are not represented in the viewbook.

- Compose different or opposing verbal passages describing characteristics of college culture that are not represented in the viewbook.
- Describe alternative visual images that are not represented in the viewbook.
- List the cultural values that these different or opposing words/phrases, passages, and images imply. (The ideal college, alternatively, should . . .)

Critique the cultural values in the viewbook from the perspective of one or more alternative discourses (freewrite).

Second, students explore how their viewbook produces certain student identities, and they critique these identities from potential alternative perspectives. The heuristic for this second critical operation follows:

Ideal Students

Analyze the viewbook's description of ideal students (brainstorm):

- List key words/phrases in the viewbook that describe ideal students.
- Transcribe verbal passages from the viewbook that describe ideal students.
- List adjectives that characterize the ideal students pictured in the viewbook's visual representations.
- List the characteristics of the ideal students that these words/phrases, passages, and adjectives imply. (The ideal college student should . . .)

Identify and describe alternative students to those represented in the viewbook (brainstorm):

- List different or opposing key words/phrases that describe students not represented in the viewbook.
- Compose different or opposing verbal passages that describe students not represented in the viewbook.

- List different or opposing adjectives that characterize students not pictured in the viewbook's visual representations.
- List the characteristics of alternative students that these different or opposing words/phrases, passages, and adjectives imply. (The ideal college student, alternatively, should . . .)

Critique the ideal students represented in the viewbook from the perspective of one or more alternative kinds of students (freewrite).

Third, students explore how their viewbook produces certain social values, and they critique these values from potential alternative perspectives. The heuristic for this third critical operation follows:

Social Values Outside the College

Analyze the viewbook's description of social values (brainstorm):

- List the key words/phrases in the viewbook that describe society outside the college.
- Transcribe verbal passages in the viewbook that describe society outside the college.
- Describe visual images in the viewbook that represent society outside the college.
- List the social values that these words/phrases, passages, and images imply. (The ideal society should . . .)

Identify alternative social values not represented in the viewbook (brainstorm):

- List different or opposing key words/phrases that are not represented in the viewbook.
- Compose different or opposing verbal passages that describe a society (or societies) not represented in the viewbook.
- Describe alternative visual images that represent a society (or societies) not represented in the viewbook.

- List the social values that these different or opposing words/phrases, passages, and images imply. (The ideal society, alternatively, should . . .)

Critique the social values in the viewbook from the perspective of one or more potential alternative discourses (freewrite).

Fourth, students explore how their viewbook produces certain social citizen identities, and they critique these identities from potential alternative perspectives. The heuristic for this fourth critical operation follows:

Ideal Social Citizens

Analyze the viewbook's description of ideal social citizens (brainstorm):

- List key words/phrases in the viewbook that describe ideal social citizens (not current students, but possibly graduates) outside the college.
- Transcribe verbal passages from the viewbook that describe ideal social citizens outside the college.
- List adjectives that characterize the ideal social citizens pictured in the viewbook's visual representations.
- List the characteristics of ideal social citizens that these words/phrases, passages, and adjectives imply. (The ideal social citizen should . . .)

Identify alternative social citizens to those represented in the viewbook (brainstorm):

- List different or opposing key words/phrases that describe social citizens not represented in the viewbook.
- Compose different or opposing verbal passages that describe social citizens not represented in the viewbook.
- List different or opposing adjectives that characterize social citizens not pictured in the viewbook's visual representations.

- List the characteristics of alternative social citizens that these different or opposing words/phrases, passages, and adjectives imply. (The ideal social citizen, alternatively, should . . .)

Critique the ideal social citizens represented in the viewbook from the perspective of one or more alternative kinds of social citizens (freewrite).

As I have argued already, only writers who examine the discursive level of language will be able to compose documents that both accommodate the rhetorical conventions of institutional discourse communities and also subvert some of their values, enabling social change within these same communities. And these are the very goals of assignment two of the viewbook project. Having sharpened their "representational resources" through critical analyses of how college viewbooks construct and promote certain cultural and social values, it is now important to turn our students' energies toward "representational processes," strategies for composing documents that promote inclusive cultural and social values. Following is the assignment sheet I give students to explain their tasks in this second assignment of the viewbook project:

Assignment Two
Producing Cultural and Social Values in College Viewbooks

This assignment gives you the opportunity to construct your own cultural values, social values, and ideal identities. Write a brief viewbook (complete with visual images) for this university. But first, decide what values and identities you most want to promote, and then decide which rhetorical strategies (both verbal and visual) will best convey those values and identities.

So your tasks will be as follows . . .

1) Write at least one page of invention notes, brainstorming the cultural values, ideal students, social values, and ideal social citizens you would like to promote for this university.

2) Design a "layout" for your viewbook.

- Your viewbook should have at least five internal pages and one cover: it should devote two or three pages to establishing cultural values, one or two pages to establishing ideal students, and at least 1 page to establishing both social values and ideal social citizens.
- Each page's layout design should have the target values and ideal identities written clearly at the top of the page.
- All your layout needs to consist of right now is a series of blocked out "photograph" sections (with brief descriptions of the kinds of visual images you plan to insert) and blocked out "text" sections (with brief descriptions of the ideas you plan to write about).

3) Draft a copy of the entire viewbook for peer review.

- Your viewbook draft should be complete with finished visuals (or at least detailed descriptions of visuals) and finished text, and bring your invention and layout pages for reference.

4) Turn in the entire viewbook assignment two in a two-pocket folder.

- On the left side, include your invention notes, layout pages, and draft.
- On the right side, include your finished viewbook.

While this final turn to productive "representational processes" may seem artificial at first, the skills students learn through composing viewbooks of their own are readily transferable to other kinds of rhetorical situations. Through writing viewbooks, students learn the crucial rhetorical skills of discovering their own values and identities and translating them into functional texts. Critique alone, in other words, leaves students with the helpless feeling that their world is less than perfect, yet there is no way to change it. In assignment two of the viewbook project, however, students learn to produce texts that represent their own values and identities, not just to critique texts that promote other values and identities.

TEACHING THE VIEWBOOK PROJECT: PEDAGOGICAL CONCERNS

Teachers preparing to use assignment one in their classes need a full stock of viewbooks. They are easy to get: simply write to the registrar of any college and request application materials. The collected view-books should come from a variety of colleges and universities. I usually let my students choose among viewbooks from private and public colleges, religious and secular colleges, technical and liberal arts colleges, men's and women's colleges, selective and open admissions colleges, two-year and four-year colleges, etc. Most widely available college guides contain information that will help separate the colleges and their viewbooks into categories, but distinguishing among schools is often a complicated task since most will not fall easily into a single category. In such cases, either file these more complex viewbooks under multiple categories (e.g., religious, liberal arts, women's colleges) or file them under their most dominant characteristic. An alternative way to prepare, less burdensome for the teacher, is to conduct the viewbook assignments as a semester-long project and have students themselves choose a set of schools from a college guide, write the registrars for application information, and begin working on assignment one as soon as the materials arrive.

Developing Representational Resources

Whether they write to colleges themselves for application materials or choose their viewbooks from the teacher's own collection, students will require some time to study their materials. I usually give students a week to learn as much as they can about their viewbooks; and while they are studying their college materials, I begin the process of teaching the assignments and heuristic. I spend the first class period (or more) on the handout for assignment one of the viewbook project, explaining the key terms that will guide the students' critical writing throughout the next few weeks. In my own collection of materials, I have several copies of a single college's viewbook, Hampden-Sydney College, and I pass these out to students whom I have divided into four groups (and, depending on class size, divided these large groups into sub-groups). I assign group one the task of examining the Hampden-Sydney viewbook for "cultural values," which, at this point, I simply describe as characteristics of the ideal college community. Group two examines the viewbook for "ideal student identities," or the characteristics of those students who would function best in the community the viewbook promotes. I assign group three the task of examining the Hampden-Sydney viewbook for "social values," which I describe as characteristics of the ideal community outside the context of the college. And group four examines the viewbook for "ideal social citizen identities," or the characteristics of those people who would function best in the kind of society the college envisions for its graduates. Without further instruction (yet), students begin to examine the Hampden-Sydney viewbook in groups, discussing the assignment's key terms in connection with the viewbook's textual and visual representations. Following about thirty minutes of collaborative exploration, students then present their findings to the rest of the class, both re-defining the terms of the assignment and exemplifying them through reading passages aloud and pointing out photographs in the viewbook that support their claims.

In the next class period, I introduce the invention heuristic based on principles derived from CDA and social-process rhetorical inquiry, and we usually spend at least two class periods fully exploring its prompts and questions. The heuristic is designed to push students to a deeper level of analysis than the assignment's key terms alone can help them reach. In these two days of class, I re-establish the same groups that students worked in during the previous class period, and I distribute again the multiple copies of the Hampden-Sydney viewbook to each group. Next, I assign group one the task of working with the first segment of the heuristic, "Cultural Values Inside the College," in relation to the Hampden-Sydney viewbook, answering the questions and responding to the prompts in as much detail as they can. I ask group two to work with the second segment of the heuristic, "Ideal Students." Group three works with the third segment, "Social Values Outside the College." And group four works with the segment on "Ideal Social Citizens." Finally, students in each group prepare a brief presentation on their findings to be given toward the end of each period.

Having taken students step-by-step through the entire heuristic, showing them specific CDA-based methods for describing the values and identities promoted in a college viewbook, the students then begin work on assignment one (including the heuristic) in relation to their own chosen viewbooks. The students' own written invention notes follow a similar pattern to the exploration we conduct in class, and this in-class exploration is crucial to the pedagogical success of the heuristic, especially for first-year composition students, many of whom have never encountered a heuristic let alone a complex social-process heuristic. Some students find the heuristic difficult to work with and others find it immediately liberating. To those who find the heuristic difficult, I explain that their explorations in response to the questions are just that—explorations—and I will often sit with them individually, flipping the pages of their chosen viewbook, collaboratively exploring some of the things the heuristic directs them toward (emphasized words and phrases, the layout and content of prominent photographs, etc.).

Andy Whitehall, a student in one of my recent second-semester required first-year composition classes, wrote his heuristic inquiry notes in response to Oberlin College's viewbook. Since most of his critical essay focuses on Oberlin's cultural values and, to a lesser extent, ideal students, I represent excerpts of Andy's notes only from these first two sections of the heuristic. First, Andy explores the cultural values promoted in Oberlin's viewbook. Following are some of the key words and phrases Andy found in the text that describe Oberlin's college culture: community of scholars, enthusiasm and achievement, the basics and foundations, open-mindedness, the heady spirit of idealism, promotes diversity, tolerance, difference, offers knowledge, experience, choices, technology, etc. Although Andy quotes several passages from the viewbook on Oberlin's college culture, one in particular influenced his critical essay:

> Because Oberlinians are such a diverse group of individuals, they don't always agree on what the world's problems are, let alone on the solutions to those problems. Outsiders might look at this community and see dissension and disunity. Insiders know better. In this community the right to disagree is respected and the need to debate issues is understood—they are inherent to intellectual inquiry and academic freedom. Tolerance is highly prized at Oberlin.

As Andy flipped through the pages of the Oberlin viewbook, he noticed that almost all of the photographs, sometimes several on each page, represented Oberlin faculty and students as ethnically diverse, a quality that supported the key phrases and passages he described earlier in his exploration. Having described these phrases, passages, and photographs, Andy determined that, from Oberlin's perspective, "the ideal college culture should, above all, promote diversity and community."

Andy had a difficult time with the next part of the heuristic, which requires students to identify alternative cultural values not described in the text; it was difficult for Andy because he agreed with the values promoted in Oberlin's viewbook. Some of the alternative phrases Andy generated follow: complacence, individuality, innovation, closed-mindedness, skepticism, sameness, ignorance, etc. By way of an opposing passage and a statement of cultural value, Andy writes, "the ideal alternative college should promote individuality and intolerance." Because Andy abhors intolerance, this alternative aspect of the heuristic was difficult for him to explore; nevertheless, Andy did give it a solid effort, and this effort resulted, as we will see, in an interesting approach to his eventual critical essay—an approach he probably would not have generated had he not attempted to construct an alternative position from which to critique Oberlin's college culture. In response to the freewriting prompt at the end of this first section of the heuristic, Andy argues that the value of diversity, which he liked in Oberlin's viewbook, might be seen as promoting intolerance in the ethnic dorms sponsored on campus: "Oberlin's practice of housing people with similar interests does not necessarily encourage acceptance, but may only encourage isolation and separation." This idea, which occupies most of Andy's freewriting, also became the most prominent subject in his eventual critical essay. Andy's heuristic exploration of Oberlin's ideal students repeats some of the information he had generated in his earlier exploration of Oberlin's cultural values, yet he did go on to describe Oberlin's ideal students as willing to accept cultural differences and form strong communities.

In the following passage from his viewbook critical essay, Andy describes the Oberlin college community as "diverse" and its ideal students as "accepting." He then negotiates this cultural value and ideal identity, simultaneously finding good and bad in them.

> Above all, Oberlin College prides itself on its diversity. It boasts a well-rounded mix of students from all over the world. This diverse community ensures that every viewpoint imaginable is represented in Oberlin's microcosm. Debate among students is encouraged; however, acceptance of others' beliefs is more highly valued. One student, quoted in the viewbook, calls Oberlin "a rich environment of diversity which fosters and allows time of great change and growth of character." Oberlin has the numbers to support its claim of a diverse community: 75% Caucasian, 10% Asian American, 7% African American, and 6% international students; also, women outnumber men by 14%. Due to its impressive diversity, Oberlin is able to offer students "special interest housing" focusing on specific cultural groups (Asia House, African Heritage House, Hebrew House, and Third World House; they also have a Women's Collective). Equality of races and sexes is important in the Oberlin community. One student says the best one-word description of Oberlin is "accepting." Oberlin was one of the first colleges to admit African Americans and women, and the viewbook cites several resource guides for African Americans that list Oberlin College as an ideal environment for African American students.
>
>   This seems like the most perfect environment in which one could live. But I have to wonder why a college that prizes diversity so much would offer students segregated housing. Students who reflect Oberlin's values would not want to be housed only with people exactly like them. Diversity is great, but I think that a college full of students who embrace other cultures so whole-heartedly would want to learn all they can about these different cultures, not separate themselves from them.

Andy's first task is simply to describe the cultural values and ideal students that he believes Oberlin sets up in its viewbook, and his second task is to critique these values and identities from a defined perspective. In these paragraphs, we find that Andy considers the value of diversity itself to be a great one, but be believes that Oberlin's method of promoting it contradicts that very value itself.

Andy chose not to draw much from the heuristic questions that establish alternative cultural values and student identities, since the alternatives to diversity and acceptance were not desirable to him; instead, Andy drew from his critical freewriting in which he had negotiated a "middle" position in favor of Oberlin's multiculturalism yet critical of its practices for achieving diversity. This excerpt from Andy's critical essay demonstrates the kind of writing that comes from the convergence of CDA methodologies and social-process rhetorical inquiry—it is a kind of critique in which writers simultaneously accommodate, resist, and negotiate the values encoded into institutional discourses. Through studying the value-laden language of the Oberlin viewbook (its key words, emphasized passages, prominent visual images, etc.) as well as the values that this language excludes, Andy is able to take a well-defined critical position on Oberlin's institutional practices for promoting diversity, a critical position that Andy might not have arrived at had he not engaged the entire cycle of CDA-based social-process rhetorical inquiry.

Beth Grady, a student in the same class with Andy, wrote her heuristic exploration notes in response to Cornell University's viewbook. Since most of Beth's critical essay focuses on the social values and ideal citizen identities promoted in Cornell's viewbook, I discuss only her notes in response to the final two sections of the heuristic. First, Beth explores Cornell's social values, listing the following key words and phrases that describe the world outside the college campus, the world that Cornell students will enter following graduation: cosmopolitan, fast paced, multicultural, diverse, challenging, global society (repeated often), and turbulent. Two passages in particular influenced Beth's perspective of Cornell's social values. First, "As the world draws together, all our differences come sliding, sometimes crashing, up against one another. If you are to make a significant contribution in the coming years to continuing advancement and world cooperation, if you are to develop and utilize your full potential, you'll need to have a knowledge and an appreciation of other's cultures and expectations. And to succeed, both as an individual and as a member of this global society, you'll need to be able to negotiate from a position of understanding and good will, as well as knowledge." Second, "Employment forecasters tell us the majority of the jobs in the twenty-first century have yet to be created. In this turbulent environment the educated person is one who easily learns new skills and deftly analyzes new information. The broad perspective you need to carry you confidently through the changes and upheavals of the upcoming century is one grounded firmly in the liberal arts." While Beth acknowledged that some sections of text in the viewbook tried to dispel the belief that Cornell is just for "rich kids," she believed that the photographs told a different story: "Some of the pictures show students on expensive ski trips, and most of them are wearing clothes that I could never afford. I like how a lot of the pictures show people from different backgrounds, but I can't really relate to the expensive preppy styles." Based on her brainstorming so far, Beth concluded that, according to Cornell's viewbook, "the ideal society is multicultural and challenging."

Unlike Andy, Beth had no trouble constructing alternative social values from which to critique Cornell's viewbook. Some of Beth's alternative key words and phrases include the following: community-based, relaxed, focused, and practical, etc. Alternative photographs might have shown, according to Beth, "real people in real work environments." By way of an alternative passage and statement of social values, Beth writes, "the ideal society, alternatively, should focus on improving local communities through focused and practical education, since without strong communities there is only social chaos." Beth's critical freewriting, which served as an early draft for one section of her critical essay, focuses largely on the alienation Beth felt as she roamed through the pages of Cornell's viewbook. Interestingly, Cornell's overt disclaimers about social class, which Beth hadn't seen in any other viewbook, meant to her that Cornell had something to hide. It is clear from her critical essay, however, that her position is conflicted on the issue of class at Cornell, since toward the end of her essay she seems to desire the lifestyle of Cornell graduates but believes she (and many others) would never achieve it. Beth's exploration of Cornell's ideal social citizens repeats some of the values she describes above, but she did find some new key words and passages that described Cornell graduates as highly intellectual and worldly.

In the following passage from her viewbook critical essay, Beth describes Cornell University's vision of society as "multicultural," "fast paced," and "challenging," with ideal citizens who are "worldly," "highly intellectual," and do not get bogged down in the mundane concerns of working-class life. She then critiques these social values and identities from a working-class perspective.

> Cornell values international cultures, displaying great pride in its study abroad programs, language houses, and multicultural campus. Cornell focuses on these other cultures because it believes its graduates will enter a world with multi-national possibilities. Cornell alumni will be leisure travelers, own international businesses, and hold political offices that require multicultural social skills. Cornell also expects its graduates to be intellectually prepared to conquer the world, or at least participate in a fast-paced lifestyle. It is obvious from the viewbook that intelligence is the key to success in the "real world," according to Cornell's social values. Most of the pictures in the viewbook focus on intellectual life and reflect international values.
>
> While Cornell's social values are perfect for students from wealthy families, they would not appeal to the average American. Most people go to college with the expectation of being prepared for the practical realities of everyday life. But for Cornell graduates, everyday life includes appreciating the Moscow Symphony Orchestra, jetting to Paris for coffee, and attending fundraising benefits for the Metropolitan Museum of Art, hardly practical realities for most people. These experiences are wonderful, but they do not describe the real working lives of most Americans.

First, Beth describes the social values and ideal social citizens represented in Cornell's viewbook, and next she critiques these values and identities from an alternative, middle-class perspective. In this passage, Beth draws heavily from her invention notes regarding the social values and ideal social citizen identities promoted in the Cornell viewbook, and Beth's critique derives largely from her identification of alternative values and identities. Beth's CDA-based social-process rhetorical inquiry led her to a critical position that she might not have otherwise articulated. From the very beginning, Beth was not attracted to the upper-class social values encoded in the key words, passages, and visual images of Cornell's viewbook, and in our conversations during the early stages of the assignment, she would couch her descriptions of these values in veiled sarcasm, which (though it has its place) is not an appropriate rhetorical strategy for academic critical writing. The heuristic encouraged Beth *first* to focus on developing a complex understanding of Cornell's values (i.e., from Cornell's perspective, not hers) and *second* to develop her own critical perspective on these values. Before working through the heuristic, Beth was quick to criticize, and not to critique, Cornell's social values, but the heuristic encouraged a more balanced, negotiated position from which Beth could compose her critical essay. CDA-based social-process rhetorical inquiry, in other words, moves students beyond "knee-jerk" responses to institutional discourses that might simply reify existing values (Andy's initial "sounds good to me" response) or offend potential audiences (Beth's initial "they're a bunch of rich kids" response) toward more balanced, multi-perspectival responses that guide effective critical writing and lead to rhetorical interventions that seek to enact social change.

Developing Representational Processes

Having completed the heuristic and critical essay in relation to their chosen viewbooks, developing a stock of "representational resources," as Kress calls them, students then proceed to assignment two of the viewbook project in which they develop "representational processes," the pragmatic skills needed to actually compose the kinds of documents they have just critiqued. In this second assignment of the viewbook project, students write a viewbook of their own for the school they currently attend.

Students begin assignment two of the viewbook project by developing a detailed page of invention notes, listing the cultural values, student identities, social values, and social citizen identities that they believe should rightly be promoted by the school they attend. The invention notes at this point should include all of the values and identities that the students can think of, good and bad, relevant and not relevant. The task of choosing the best values and identities to promote in their own viewbooks will come later. The goal here is to generate as many potential choices as possible. I have seen many students restrict their invention to only those details they considered relevant to their project, then shift the focus of their project leaving them with little useful invention.

Having brainstormed lists of values and identities and narrowed their choices to the best few, students then begin the process of designing their viewbooks. I usually have students browse through many different kinds of viewbooks at this point, helping them develop further representational resources beyond those they discovered through the critical part of the viewbook project. As a sort of "pre-draft" planning exercise, I have students construct "layout pages" for their proposed viewbook. These layout pages are not really drafts, since students do not need any actual visual images or finished text yet; these pages simply help students "see" the whole project before they begin the process of composing text and developing images. The main goals here are, first, to make sure that the planned text-sections and images interact well to promote the target values and identities, and second, to avoid repetition among the different pages of the planned viewbook.

The next task students undertake is the draft of the entire viewbook, complete with texts and visuals. The visual images and text segments should be generated together; it is difficult to compose all of the text segments and then find images that interact well with them, and it is poor rhetorical strategy to compose texts based solely on available images. Students bring their completed drafts in to class for peer review with the targeted cultural values, ideal student identities, social values, and ideal social citizens written at the top of each draft page. I then have students peer review each other's drafts, and they revise their drafts into finished projects according to the review comments they receive.

In their effort to establish desirable cultural values and ideal student identities for East Carolina University, values based on cultural diversity, Jacky Taylor and John Banks wrote the following passage for their viewbook:

> East Carolina University is a public school which seeks people of all backgrounds to enrich its campus culture. ECU prides itself on its cultural diversity, since a diverse environment helps create well-rounded individuals. Cultural diversity is evident in many places on ECU's campus. There are different organizations students can join, such as the Women's Studies Alliance and the Thespians of Diversity, and many of the courses also focus on issues of diversity. Further, students with disabilities are encouraged to participate fully in ECU's campus culture: the entire campus is wheelchair accessible and the university supplies sign language interpreters at no cost to hearing-disabled students. Opportunities and access are the keys to ECU's diversity, and there are always interesting things to do when you need a break from studying.

This passage is accompanied in the viewbook by a photograph of a professor in a wheelchair making a vigorous and entertaining argument to students from a variety of ethnic backgrounds. Jacky and John had two things in mind as they composed the passage: 1) that they appreciate the many activities promoting diversity on the ECU campus, and 2) that the student population itself is not diverse enough, so a certain degree of recruiting would benefit the university. The strategies that Jacky and John employ to accomplish these rhetorical goals include listing several things about ECU that foster diversity and also representing (photographically) a diverse student body, hoping, of course, that prospective ECU students who value diversity would be moved by their description to apply for admission.

Next, in their effort to establish desirable social values and ideal social citizen identities for East Carolina University students, values based on strong communities and citizen participation, Sam Waters and Tara Dooley wrote the following passage:

> East Carolina graduates become deeply involved in their home communities. Active communities are good communities, and ECU encourages participation in activities of all kinds. While at ECU, you might participate in club sports, academic organizations, and a variety of entertainment

events, all of which will help you gain the social skills necessary to be a leader in your community.

This passage is accompanied in the viewbook by a photograph of a group of students building a house with Habitat for Humanity. Sam and Tara believe that the skills students learn in school should last a lifetime, and that all citizens should give back as much as possible to the communities in which they live, and these values are evident in the rhetorical strategies that Sam and Tara chose for their viewbook.

Through composing their own viewbooks, many students come to realize that locating cultural and social values in institutional discourses is not only a critical enterprise; it is also a productive enterprise requiring a pre-text sense of the world inside and outside institutional contexts. An obvious benefit of this approach to composing is that it teaches students concrete ways in which their writing participates in social processes beyond academic boundaries, a goal shared by many who teach writing as a social act; a disadvantage of this approach for some students, of course, is that it is a much more difficult way to compose than the traditional pre-write, write, rewrite advice we find in many of our composition textbooks. While my students always invent, compose, and revise their essays, they also engage in a kind of social-process rhetorical inquiry that locates writing (their writing) in discursive processes, in cycles of cultural production, contextual distribution, and critical consumption.

Students who complete both assignments one and two of the viewbook project, then, engage the writing process in its fullest sense. Each student's goal in these assignments is not, however, to become a "cultural critic," but rather to enter into a dialogue with institutional texts and contexts, both critiquing and producing discourses from their own defined perspectives (even if those perspectives contradict everything a "cultural critic" might believe). In my experience, students, having begun to expand their warehouses of representational resources and processes through CDA-based social-process rhetorical inquiry, quickly develop the ability to analyze and critique the exigencies of complex rhetorical situations and respond in writing to those exigencies. Through these viewbook assignments, composition students come to realize even more that individual texts participate in larger contexts of institutional discourses, discourses that are steeped in cultural and social values, and the success of any text relies ultimately on its interactions within these discursive environments.

NOTES

1. I call systemic and functional linguistics "rhetorical" because Halliday himself views them that way. In *Spoken and Written Language*, in fact, Halliday laments that traditional linguistics has divorced language structure from language use, and he reminds us that "historically, the study by which issues of use had been most effectively addressed had been that of rhetoric" (vi).

2. Most recently, Hodge and Kress published *Social Semiotics*, a companion volume to their much earlier *Language as Ideology*, and Kress has extended his work into composition studies with *Learning to Write* and *Writing the Future*. Fowler's most recent work, such as *Language in the News*, centers on critical analyses of the ideological work performed by "objective" news discourse.

CHAPTER SIX

Writing in Context

MOST WRITING TEACHERS AGREE THAT THEIR COURSES PREPARE students for "life" in the "real world," but few teachers have theorized what sort of "life" they wish for their students, and even fewer describe the condition of this "real world." Yet, these are crucial tasks that those in academia cannot ignore. "Life" implies *activity*, and "real world" implies a *context* for that activity. Thus, in terms of writing instruction: 1) teachers ought to articulate the kinds of activities they want their students to perform outside the classroom, and they should design pedagogical techniques that develop skills in their students consistent with these future activities; 2) teachers ought to theorize the nature of the social context within which these activities will be performed, and they should design curricula based on the structures and processes that comprise this context; and 3) teachers ought to predict the positive and negative effects these activities in these future contexts might have on both students and society alike. As Gunther Kress convincingly argues,

> A curriculum is a design for a future social subject, and via that envisioned subject a design for a future society. That is, the curriculum puts forward knowledges, skills, meanings, values in the present which will be telling in the lives of those who experience the curriculum ten or twenty years later. Forms of pedagogy experienced by children now in school suggest to them forms of social relations which they are encouraged to adopt, adapt, modify and treat as models. The curriculum, and its associated pedagogy, puts forward a set of cultural, linguistic and social resources . . . in relation to which (among others) students constantly

construct, reconstruct and transform their subjectivity. Such a view of the curriculum and of pedagogy requires . . . that those who construct the curriculum have a vision of the future in which this subject, here and now experiencing the curriculum, will lead her or his life—a culturally, personally, socially productive life, one hopes. ("Representational" 16)

In this chapter, I argue that the nature of the social context within which our students will "live" their lives is best described as "postmodern," and, a little later in this chapter, I describe a series of writing assignments designed to develop in students certain skills they will need to "live" in this postmodern "real world."

POSTMODERNITY, COMMUNAL DEMOCRACIES, AND THE FUNCTIONS OF RHETORIC

According to Jean-François Lyotard, postmodernity "designates the state of our culture following the transformations which, since the end of the nineteenth century, have altered the game rules of science, literature, and the arts" (*Postmodern* xxiii). These new postmodern "game rules," as Stanley Aronowitz suggests, are "marked by the renunciation of foundational thought" (99). More specifically, postmodern theorists critique modernist foundational thought on three fronts: first, they scorn the interpretive pursuit of universal meaning "re-presented" by verbal and visual codes, favoring instead a semiotics of surface and context; second, they describe the dissolution of the unified subject into networks of dissonant discursive formations and contradictory subject positions; and third, they reject universal (master, grand) narratives and structures of legitimation, opting instead for localized legitimation at the level of community. In postmodern culture, in other words, there is no universal foundation, no immutable Truth upon which to base language, self, and society. There are only probabilities generated within communal constraints.

But traditional accounts of rhetoric (and, later, composition) from ancient Greece throughout much of the twentieth century have accepted the following (anachronistically "modernist") Aristotelian formulation: science, literature, and, in particular, philosophy operate in the realm of Truth; rhetoric, in the form of political, legal, and ceremonial discourses, operates in the realm of probability. So what happens to these Aristotelian accounts of rhetoric's scope when modernist Truth itself is renounced? Under such postmodern circumstances, all realms of human experience—whether scientific or legal, philosophical or political, aesthetic or ceremonial—fall into the realm of rhetoric, and all signifying practices, both verbal and visual, are necessarily socio-politically motivated.

Certain modernist critics understand postmodern theorists' skeptical and relativistic world-views as limited critical attitudes in which the very possibility for political action is destroyed. In a postmodern world of relative truths, fractured subjectivities, and localized modes of legitimation, these modernist critics argue, political projects are rendered impotent because their required foundations simply do not exist. Political projects, they argue, require foundations—absolute Truth and accurate re-presentations of it, unified and hierarchized subjects, and universal narratives and structures of legitimation—in order to be viable in the "real" world of social practices (Norris 1-45, for example). According to these modernists, those who have legitimated access to Truth (naturally) rule those who do not. Such foundational political ideals, however, are abhorrent to postmodern cultural theorists who value democracy over meritocracy.

Democratic postmodern theorists, especially Jean-François Lyotard, Henry Giroux, Ernesto Laclau and Chantal Mouffe, and, in his more recent work, Jacques Derrida, advocate a politics of what I will call "communal democracies" over other forms of government.[1] Political systems conceived as "communal democracies" require that all members of every community, from international institutions to individual family units, represent politically their communal concerns from competing subject positions to interested citizens in equally powerful subject positions, and these political systems require that divergent representations be legitimated through paralogy, competing discourses about the future of a community. These communal democracies do not attempt to cross cultural boundaries—there are no universal, trans-social "laws," since every culture experiences unique material conditions and represents its world differently. It is this political possibility of communal democracy opened up by postmodern critical attitudes that lends significance to postmodern social practices; and it is the goal of effective participation in radical democracies that must inform postmodern writing instruction.

Within this context of postmodern communal democracies, each participating citizen must possess two general skills that enable democratic activity: first, the ability to *critique* marginalizing representations, disadvantageous subject positions, and biased modes of legitimation; second, the ability to *compose* empowering representations, advantageous subject positions, and yet remain inside the scope of "legitimate" discursive practices within any given institution. Both of these skills, critiquing and composing, are crucial for a postmodern pedagogy, since, as John McGowan points out, "postmodernism rejects any [modernist] reliance on critique's inherent liberating powers, devoting itself instead to developing new aesthetic, textual, and political strategies to combat or undermine the monolith" (14). In postmodern pedagogies for writing instruction, then, students read and write politicized representations of their worlds from a variety of fragmented and often contradictory subject positions under unique constraints of localized modes of legitimation; students critique the production, distribution, and consumption of dominant representations in specific lived cultures from alternative and often subversive subjectivities; and students accommodate, negotiate, and/or resist these representations through producing and distributing alternative representations for consumption in these lived cultures.

I designed the composition pedagogy that I present in this chapter to take account of my students' and my own cultural worlds as predominantly postmodern—as a multiplicity of identifiably distinct though inevitably interdependent communities in which citizens, occupying varied and often contradictory subject positions in institutional power formations, represent their worlds politically through language for audiences (other citizens in different subject positions) who legitimate or delegitimate representations according to localized rhetorical norms. Each of these communities has its own power hierarchies, and the goals of the pedagogy I describe here include preparing students to participate in the flow of discourse that generates localized institutional knowledge, i.e., to participate in the discursive practices that characterize and encourage communal democracies.

My first task in designing the postmodern composition curriculum described here was to decide collaboratively with my students what socio-cultural "institutions," broadly conceived—such as churches and religions, schools and systems of education, media technologies, family units, workplaces and unions, political parties and interest groups, etc.—most affect their lives. For example, students attending a college with a firm religious affiliation may be more concerned with religious institutions than students attending a secular school; and students attending a vocational college may be more concerned with workplaces and unions than students attending a liberal arts college, etc. During two recent semesters, my students and I chose to center our composition courses around institutions of higher learning—institutions with which all of my students had extensive experience. And we called these courses "Writing in Context: Education."

Once we had chosen the institution around which our classes would center, the next step was to design the specific writing assignments students would complete, assignments that would teach students to critique and compose representations, subjectivities, and modes of legitimation in ways that would foster their participation in postmodern communal democracies. To these ends, for each writing assignment in "Writing in Context: Education," students first critiqued some aspect of their own lived-experience in institutions of higher learning, and then they composed positive rhetorical documents designed to address the problems raised in their critiques.

Critical Position Statements

But this initial "critical discourse" required in each major writing assignment in "Writing in Context: Education" is not a natural one for most students. Thus, students began the term writing position statements in response to readings that dealt with a variety of educational issues: one position statement, for example, was on "cultural literacy" in response to selections from E. D. Hirsch's *Cultural Literacy;* another was on "problem-posing" education in response to selections from Paulo Freire's *Pedagogy of the Oppressed;* and another was on "hidden curriculum" in response to selections from Theodore Sizer's *Horace's Compromise.* In her position statement, Dana Semann, one of the students in the class, writes that Hirsch's notion of cultural literacy is important and needs to be addressed in schools ("otherwise, everything's an inside joke"); however, she disagrees with Hirsch that the body of knowledge that constitutes "cultural literacy" should remain the same across generations and social borders. For Dana, "cultural literacy" means the ability to communicate (via a shared body of knowledge) within particular cultures, and Hirsch's attempt to establish a nation-wide body of knowledge is unnecessary and unrealistic. Dana approaches Hirsch's text as a politicized representation to be interpreted but not to be accepted without critical consideration. Bill Ackerman argues that Freire's notion of problem-posing education would work for advanced students; however, there would need to be a point in students' educations when they memorized facts. Problem-posing, in other words, cannot function until there is a base of knowledge with which to work—with which, that is, to pose problems. Bill also objects to Sizer's characterization of American high schools and their students. For Bill, who attended four different high schools, Sizer simplifies (through his use of universalizing narrative) a number of complex issues just to prove his points: "Sizer's account, probably intended to be a realistic description of the average high school and the average student, ends up only creating stereotypes." Bill argues that his own experiences were quite different from those Sizer wrote about: "Maybe it's just been too long since he's been in high school," Bill writes, "because it sure wasn't like that when I went." For Bill, both Freire and Sizer politically represent educational issues from particular ideological perspectives—perspectives that were not necessarily the same as his own.

In their position statements, both Dana and Bill establish their own positions on cultural literacy, problem-posing education, and hidden curriculum in dialectical interaction with the selections they read on these issues. In other words, they develop their own positions through a process of accommodating, resisting, and negotiating (from their own perspectives which they developed through lived experience in various educational cultures) the arguments in the readings. As Richard Johnson points out, postmodern cultural studies uses critique in productive ways, as "a kind of alchemy for producing useful knowledge" (38). In these students' position statements, the critical reading process is a productive one, a process in which the readers construct their own positions on issues through dialectical interaction with "other" perspectives. These students do not simply accept or reject ideas based on a predetermined universal narrative or structure; rather, they negotiate meaning, constructing in the process new meaning, localized meaning. The positions that Dana and Bill developed through their critical readings of Hirsch, Freire, and Sizer became starting-points for more involved critical essays, essays which required them to critique their own educational experiences from their own articulated positions on cultural literacy, problem-posing education, and hidden curriculum. These critical position statements, then, served as invention heuristics designed to direct students toward more extended critical efforts.

First Writing Assignment

In the first major writing assignment, students were given two general tasks, one critical and the other pragmatic: "first, you will write an individual essay demonstrating 'critical awareness' of the purpose and character of high school education and how it differs from college education; second, you will write a *High School Student's Guide to College Preparation* (hereafter HSS Guide) in which you suggest ways that students can best use their time to prepare for higher education." As a guide to the critical portion of this writing assignment, I provided students with the following heuristic:

Heuristic: Critical Awareness

The goal of the first part of this writing assignment is to let you examine critically your own high school and college experiences. Compare, contrast, and critique your high school(s) and "X" University based on the kinds of knowledge they attempt to foster (logic, problem solving, memorization, quantitative math and science vs. qualitative English and history, etc.) and the kinds of practical skills they attempt to develop (writing, typing, wood or metal working, public speaking, etc.) in their students.

From your perspective, then:

- What kinds of knowledge and skills from your high school experience prepared you best for college?
- What knowledge and skills have not transferred into your college experience?
- What kinds of teaching (cultural literacy, problem-posing) are practiced at your high school and at "X" University?
- What are the hidden curricula at your high school and at "X" University?
- What might you have done differently in high school to prepare better for college?

In his critical essay on the transition from high school to college, Scott Holt, an Education major, argues that the hidden curriculum of his high school exercised a degree of moral control over its students, moral control that did not allow students to develop certain practical skills they would need in college. For example, in Scott's high school, teachers assumed that students would not do homework unless they were tested frequently; but frequent testing, according to Scott, eliminated the need for skills such as note taking. Scott puts it this way: "The difference is that in my high school, tests came about every-other week, and in college there are only two or three a semester. I didn't need to take notes in high school to remember what was said in class. But in college, where I'm only in the classroom two or three times a week, taking notes is vital to studying for the few tests we have." According to Scott, the desire for moral control over students through frequent testing is noticeably absent in college (though Scott is quick to point out that moral control is present in other forms such as attendance policies and classroom etiquette), and students like Scott are left to their own devices to develop the skills their teachers neglected (consciously or not) in high school.

Critique, however, is not the sole or even primary object of postmodern writing instruction. Preparing students for participation in postmodern communal democracies entails providing students with critical cultural knowledge as well as practical rhetorical skills with which to apply that knowledge. For if critical knowledge never enters the flow of public discourse, then it perishes in the silence of its knower. In postmodern writing instruction, then, students compose discourses that attempt to solve the problems foregrounded in their cultural critiques.

For the second (practical) part of this first writing assignment, Scott composed a pamphlet for students at his high school, and I provided him (and the rest of the students in the class) with the following prompt as a guide:

> Write a *High School Student's Guide to College Preparation* (*HSS Guide*) for your high school(s). Use what you have learned in the "critical" part of the assignment to guide your writing here. This HSS Guide should, at the very least: profile high school, profile college, and suggest ways high school students might best use their time to prepare for higher education.
>
> Remember, this HSS Guide should not criticize the way things are done in the schools—instead it should suggest ways high school students (most likely in their freshman and sophomore years) can enhance their abilities to succeed in college.
>
> Write this guide as a pamphlet; that is, combine written text with visual images to create an overall effect. You might also include things like short checklists of things to do and brief lists of "tidbit" advice. Your style should reflect the interests of young high school students.

Scott's high school's hidden curriculum prevented him from gaining effective note-taking skills; thus, based on his critical essay on the transition from high school to college, and the difficulties he himself had, Scott chose to focus on note taking in his *HSS Guide* (which also included a number of other subjects as well). Under the heading "Note taking," Scott suggests that high school students try the following note taking methods in preparation for college, even if they do not feel the need for them in their high school classes:

- Use different color pens for different kinds of information (use red for major points or summaries and black for details and facts)
- Write major points and summaries on the far-left margin and indent details and facts
- Always write legibly and correct errors carefully so your notes make sense when you read them later
- Develop and make a master list of shorthand abbreviations for the key terms in each lecture
- Copy your notes into another notebook as soon after a lecture as you can—you'll remember more of what you couldn't write during class, and you'll be able to fill in details you might have otherwise forgotten

These methods, Scott argues, not only make the note taking process faster, but they also make notes easier to study after they have been taken. Even though high school students would rarely find a use for so elaborate a system for note taking (because the moral codes in the hidden curriculum of Scott's high school devalued long-term knowledge), Scott felt that if students in his high school practiced these methods, then the transition from high school to college classes would be easier; and new college students who already know how to take notes effectively will get more academic benefit from their freshman year than students who do not know how to take notes.

Scott uses his *HSS Guide* as a way of addressing the problems he describes in his critical analysis of the transitions from high school to college; he politically represents his own problems in making this transition and then composes a document that attempts to alleviate those problems for other members of his high school community. Scott constructs and occupies a powerful subject position (as a former high school student who had made it through the difficult experience of going to college) in his HSS Guide, and the rhetorical purpose of this guide is to empower the subjectivities of future college students in his high school community.

Second Writing Assignment

For the second writing assignment in "Writing in Context: Education," students again confronted politicized representations, fragmented subjectivities, and localized modes of legitimation. This next assignment, like the first, has two parts: first, students write a critical evaluation of their academic major; second, they write a letter to the Head of their department or program suggesting curricular changes based on the findings in their critiques. Students were provided with the following prompt to guide their critical analyses:

> Part I of this assignment includes three tasks:
>
> First, write a detailed account of the university requirements (the formal curriculum) for a major in your field: What courses are required (how many and at what level)? What electives are allowed? What practical (teaching, lab) requirements must you fulfill? Why are these requirements necessary to be a(n) "X" major? What purposes do they serve? What kinds of knowledge and skills are foregrounded in the requirements for your major?
>
> Second, write a detailed account of what people who have graduated in your major are doing: What jobs do they get? What do they need to know to do these jobs? What practical skills must they have to do these jobs? You should interview at least three people who have careers in fields related to your major and discuss these interviews in your essay.
>
> Third, critique your major curriculum: what aspects of the requirements for your major prepare students for life beyond college and what aspects do not and thus need to be revised.

Michael Casnellie, a Genetic Bioengineering major in the Interdisciplinary Engineering program, began this assignment with a unique problem: his major did not have a set formal curriculum. According to Michael, Genetic Bioengineering majors take thirty credit hours required for all Engineering majors by the Schools of Engineering, which most Genetic Bioengineering students register for during their freshman year. From that point on, however, there are few guidelines. Genetic Bioengineering majors write their own plans of study (a long and tedious process) during their sophomore years. In his critical essay, Michael writes, "There are no decent sample plans of study, and since no professors or counselors graduated with degrees in GB [Genetic Bioengineering] there are few resources for us to consult." In this essay, Michael describes the plan of study that he devised during his sophomore year, explaining his reasons for its organization. However, Michael recounts, "It wasn't till after I wrote my plan of study that I started to learn about medical school and the requirements to get in." Michael found that the plan of study he had written and filed with the Schools of Engineering was not what most medical schools he had researched wanted to see. Michael then revised his plan of study into one that he thought was perfect for him as a Genetic Bioengineering major: each semester had a manageable workload and contained a variety of subjects, making high GPAs possible, and the plan of study foregrounded Humanities courses, which medical schools feel improves prospective students' potential abilities to communicate effectively with patients.

For the second (pragmatic) part of this writing assignment, Michael wrote a letter to the Chair of the Interdisciplinary Engineering programs. In this letter, Michael writes: "While the tremendous flexibility is what initially lured me to Genetic Bioengineering, guidance for creating a well organized plan of study could be improved, especially for pre-med students." One solution that Michael suggests is to provide freshmen in Genetic Bioengineering with plans of study developed by current majors, so Michael included a copy of his own revised plan of study with his letter and granted the Chair of the Interdisciplinary Engineering programs permission to distribute copies of it to the Engineering advising staff. Michael mailed this letter after writing it, and a few weeks later he received a note from the Chair of the Interdisciplinary Engineering programs thanking Michael for his help and assuring him that the sample plan of study would circulate to the appropriate faculty members and students.

Michael found that no available representations of the Genetic Bioengineering major were adequate for students to follow, and new ones needed to be developed. While Michael did not occupy a subject position from which he himself could directly solve the problems Genetic Bioengineering majors faced in developing their plans of study, he certainly did occupy a subject position that merited attention within the Interdisciplinary Engineering program discourse community. As a student in the program, Michael was able to point out problems that professors and administrators did not encounter, problems which harmed the community as a whole, and problems which a number of different members of the community eventually worked to alleviate. Michael was surprised when the Chair of the Interdisciplinary Engineering programs actually accepted his advice. But Michael realized that when he constructed his subject position as a member of a communal democracy, his proposed changes were accorded more credence, his discourse was legitimated according to the specific communal needs of the Genetic Bioengineering program.

Third Writing Assignment

This third writing assignment turned students' attention toward formal and hidden academic cultures. The following is the assignment handout that I distributed to my students:

School Critical and Practical Essays: Assignments

In these essays, you will examine the culture of "school" critically. We are all students; school affects us every day, whether we are on campus or at home studying. Our high schools and colleges have a tremendous influence on our development into adults. It is crucial, therefore, that we understand critically the ways in which schools condition us to be certain kinds of people. Only then are we able to choose for ourselves whether or not to accept the roles our schools would like us to occupy.

This assignment has two parts: first, a critical evaluation of the formal and hidden curricula in one class you have completed in the last year or so; and second, a practical letter to either the teacher of the class or an administrator at the school. The critical essay should describe problems you encountered in the formal and hidden curricula, and the practical letter should attempt to resolve some of those problems.

School Critical Essay

In this essay, you will be writing about a class you have recently had, and one from which you have kept some materials (syllabus, course policies, handouts, the textbook, etc.). Although much of what you write in this essay will come from your own memory, these course materials will help you "document" the experience. In both the critical and practical essays, please remove all references to the teacher's name and the specific division and section number of the course in which you were enrolled.

Your audience for the school critical essay should be university students who have not taken the particular class you describe. Assume, in other words, that your audience knows a lot about this university generally but nothing at all about your own experience in the class about which you have chosen to write.

School Practical Essay

Once you have thoroughly critiqued the formal and hidden curricula of the class you have chosen as the focus for your critical essay, write a letter either to the teacher of the class or to an administrator at the school. This letter should propose improvements to the existing formal and hidden curricula. Be sure to adopt a proper tone for your audience.

After introducing the school critical and practical essay assignments, I next acquaint students with the critical context that will guide them in their school essays. I provide a handout that describes formal and hidden curricula and includes a few basic heuristic prompts students use as invention guides for exploring their experiences in school (see Appendix A).

While discussing this handout, students come to realize that teachers represent the formal curricula of their courses in political ways through hidden curriculum strategies, and students consume these hidden curriculum strategies from a multiplicity of equally political subjectivities, resulting in widely varying evaluative accounts of a single course. In their critical essays, students construct their subjectivities both as members of a localized community (the community of a single class) and as members of a more generalized community (their own university) toward whom, and for the benefit of whom, their critiques—their politicized representations—are directed. And in their practical essays, students direct their critical discourse toward an individual in the institution itself (whether the teacher in question or an administrator higher up in the university's power hierarchy) who has the potential to change the institutional processes that result in marginalizing hidden curriculum strategies, thereby legitimating new institutional practices that benefit the local and general communities in question.

Once students have studied the assignment and invention handouts, I begin a series of classroom activities that lead students to a more critical understanding of how schools politically represent and legitimate certain subjectivities. We start these activities by reviewing and discussing again the readings by Sizer, Hirsch, and Freire. Through these readings and our discussion of them, students develop a critical sense that school is not necessarily the warehouse of Truths they might have thought it was; they come to understand that the function of school is only partly to impart content knowledge, but also partly to instill in students certain advantageous communal values and mold students into productive citizens of both local and global communities. Following what is often a vigorous discussion of these readings, I then continue with a class discussion of my own formal curriculum and hidden curriculum strategies.

This discussion is usually awkward for my students and me: most of my students, at this point in their academic lives, have only recently come to recognize some of the social powers exerted on them in school, and they are reluctant to "accuse" me of such manipulations. However, acknowledging my position within the academic hierarchy, I suggest to my students that I do in fact use hidden curriculum strategies to "encourage" them to be certain kinds of citizens in our classroom community. And in order to demonstrate my hidden curriculum to them, I usually begin with an explanation of my attendance policy and why I restrict the number of absences that I allow my students to take. According to my attendance policy, I give students a "cushion" of four absences, beyond which every two additional absences lower their final course grade a full letter. Many college students find attendance policies unnecessarily restrictive, and they are quick to describe them as methods for controlling student behavior. And they're right. I explain that I consider good attendance to be a distinguishing mark of good students—those who succeed in educational institutions are the ones who attend classes regularly, and I have decided (somewhat arbitrarily, I must admit) that less than five absences equals "regular" attendance. In fact, I have failed students with "excessive absences" (according to my policy), even though all of their assignments received passing grades. I also tend to reward students with perfect attendance. When a student's final grade is on the border, I consider perfect attendance reason enough to move the student to a higher grade. Students often point out to me (and I had not thought of it this way until my students pointed it out) that I make "good" students out of those who attend and "bad" students out of those who do not; they argue that sometimes students' attendance reflects as much in my grading practices as their actual ability to write well.

During this class discussion, which soon moves on to other topics, I record on the chalk board as much as I can of what my students say, and I never defend my own formal or hidden curricula; I will, however, try to give students reasons for my pedagogical practices. But my goal is to encourage critique, and I find that students are willing to engage me in this exercise even though I remain in a position of institutional power over them. Soon we examine the entire invention heuristic and apply it generally to our composition class. Students critique the geographical design of the classroom, for example, exploring how its physical layout implies certain relationships between students and their teachers. In one of my classrooms, three progressively raised tiers of long, curved tables are set in semi-circles around a pit with a podium from which the teacher lectures. Since the students' chairs are bolted to the floor, there are no other arrangements possible for their seating; and since the first and lowest semi-circular table (at which few students ever sit) blocks off the rest of the classroom from the pit and the podium, there are few opportunities for teachers to interact personally with students. This classroom, students argue, places teachers inevitably in positions of power, whether they want the power or not, and students, out of sheer geographical intimidation, adopt passive subjectivities. Through this group discussion of my own hidden curriculum and that implied in the arrangement of the classroom itself, students learn to critique school as an institution that constructs politicized representations implying particular subjectivities arranged in definite power hierarchies that are reinforced and legitimated through (sometimes arbitrary) social practices.

Toward the end of this class discussion, I open the floor to suggestions for improving my formal and hidden curriculum practices. Inevitably, some students vote to abolish attendance requirements and grant all of them the A's they "deserve." But they usually realize that such suggestions result in oppositional responses and prevent serious change. Most students offer more tempered suggestions, such as taking into account individual cases when recording absences in my grade book (which I actually do, but I do not tell them about it until later in the semester), or such as allowing students to sit on the floor and stairs in the classroom instead of in the fixed seats/desks that place them immediately in an inferior position in relation to me. I often accept many of these suggestions and throughout the rest of the course I draw attention to instances when I consciously follow their advice. When I do not accept students' advice on a question of formal or hidden curriculum, I explain my reasoning and invoke my power to continue my usual pedagogical practices.

With this in-class experience under their belts, I find that students are able to critique successfully a variety of other classes they have taken in the recent past; their experience with an "addressed" audience (me) tells them much about how they need to approach their "invoked" audiences (past teachers and/or administrators). Following are two passages from one student's critical essay on the formal and hidden curriculum of a course she had taken while in college. Regarding the formal curriculum, Susan writes:

> English 2700 is a Language Studies class, and the formal curriculum is extremely stimulating. Students in this class learn the meanings of key terms like "jargon" and "euphemism," but the focus of our lessons stemmed primarily from multiculturalism. Bilingual education, Black English, and gender issues became the most poignant topics in our classroom. The books we read and the videos we watched explained that all people have their own individual dialect, and that education systems must account for each different way of speaking and writing.

This passage constitutes a fairly objective description of the content of the course called "Language Studies." Susan does not attempt here to discuss the politics of the subject matter, and more importantly she does not discuss the teaching methods employed in conveying the course content. That comes later in the sections of Susan's critical essay on the hidden curriculum of the course in question. Regarding the hidden curriculum of "Language Studies," Susan writes:

> Ms. X was adamant about class participation, and she would randomly call on students to answer questions that usually led into heated debates. These debates were on a variety of subjects, and they usually took up the majority of class time. During such class discussions, Ms. X expressed her morals and values to the class in passionate language, and we were supposed to regard her values as superior to ours. Bilingual education became a controversial topic in our classroom, and the debate over the issue often began with Ms. X's opinion and ended with her opinion. Elizabeth, an outspoken student, believed that American school systems should not be responsible for teaching English to immigrants, and she refused to acknowledge that she lives in a multicultural society. When Ms. X heard this, she immediately began listing the benefits of bilingual education. As an advocate of multiculturalism, Ms. X proceeded to tell Elizabeth and the rest of the class that we must recognize that America is multicultural. I certainly agreed with Ms. X, but I did not think it was

necessary for her to force her beliefs on someone else. Her hidden curriculum implied that it was fine to denounce the beliefs of others rather than discover why they hold those particular beliefs. I was interested in knowing why Elizabeth felt the way she did. Instead, I watched Ms. X bombard her with facts, figures, and personal beliefs, attempting to change her opinion. But in reality, Ms. X only created an atmosphere of tension in the class that prevented many of her students from absorbing the content of the formal curriculum.

In this passage, Susan critiques the specific pedagogical practices—the hidden curriculum strategies—with which Ms. X conveys the formal curriculum of the course "Language Studies." In this course, the formal curriculum is viewed as a moral imperative, a set of beliefs that students must adopt in order to be effective citizens in a multicultural society. However, as Susan points out, there may be reasons for Elizabeth's negative view of multiculturalism; and since Ms. X's hidden curriculum strategies silenced Elizabeth, this student, now more than ever, will resist the democratic impulses that ground multicultural theory. Hidden curriculum strategies can either support or subvert a formal curriculum, and Susan's experience in "Language Studies" is an example of a hidden curriculum that subverts its formal curriculum. Ms. X's pedagogical goal, of course, is to create multiculturalists of her students, and the assigned readings and videos support that goal; but Ms. X's classroom strategy of challenging students for expressing non-multicultural beliefs only subverts her formal curriculum goal, creating tension in the classroom that negatively affected all students, not just Elizabeth.

In an attempt to solve some of the problems Susan points out in her critical essay, she then turns her sights to a practical letter addressed to Ms. X.

Susan's Letter

Dear Ms. X:

As a student in your English 2700 class last semester, I learned a great deal about the importance of multiculturalism in American education. But several students, including myself at times, were unsettled by some of your classroom practices. Just a few minor adjustments will certainly result in a more effective learning environment.

During many of our discussions of controversial topics, you often disregarded the opinions of participating students, and you also tried to impress your own opinions on other students. I truly respect you as a professor, Ms. X; however, these classroom practices may discourage your students from participating in class, and may turn them off to the content you convey in English 2700.

If you agree that this may be a potential problem, then you might try to acknowledge your students' beliefs and explore why they hold values different from your own. Please do not hesitate to contact me if you would like to discuss these matters further.

Sincerely,
Susan

The goal of critical discourse in postmodern composition classes is to construct communities more productive of democratic political processes, and Susan moves in that direction in her practical letter to Ms. X. Rather than simply complaining to Ms. X about her personality, Susan transforms her own personal critical knowledge into communal discourse, presenting the subject in her practical letter as a problem for everyone involved (both Ms. X and her students), thereby enhancing the potential for real change in future sections of English 2700. But even if Ms. X does not accept Susan's advice, it is important for students to learn that their critical knowledge is significant only insofar as it is made public.

In her critical essay and practical letter, Susan learns that representation is a political act. There is no True re-presentation of the problems in Ms. X's "Language Studies" class; there are only competing discourses. And Susan's postmodern rhetorical task is to participate in all of those discourses and mediate among them for the greater good of the community as a whole. Further, in these assignments, Susan consciously adopts two different subjectivities: in her critical essay, Susan writes as a student with a certain detached critical distance from her teacher Ms. X; in her practical letter, Susan writes in a more collegial tone indicating an alliance of values with Ms. X. And Susan shifts subjectivities consciously because she knows that if she were to write her practical letter in the same tone as her critical essay, Ms. X would dismiss Susan's arguments (de-legitimate them) as "irrational." Susan knows that self-centered, offensive language does nothing to advance students toward the goal of enacting change in real communities.

Students need to learn socio-rhetorical strategies that enlist all members of specific communities—even those who have, in their eyes, committed offenses—in a common goal to make the communities better as a whole. And it is only through the postmodern turn toward pragmatic, public discourse that students can learn these socio-rhetorical strategies. I believe that the development or awakening of "critical consciousness" *alone* (or what Paulo Freire has called *conscientização*)— i.e., the single most important goal for what has become known as "critical pedagogy"—is insufficient. It is crucial that students *also* learn to transform their critical knowledge into communal discourse, audience-centered communication with the intention of influencing cultural practices through persuasive writing. By following up their critical essays with practical letters, students not only awaken in themselves a certain critical consciousness, but they also learn the very rhetorical strategies needed to act on the critical knowledge they gain from postmodern writing assignments, and these rhetorical strategies empower students in communities they may have thought were otherwise controlled by immutable Realities and universal Truth.

CONCLUSION

Although "correctness" is an issue in all of my composition classes, I argue that there is more to effective writing than just putting commas in their proper places. This is hardly a radical claim, but I would like to take this argument a step further. Although invention, revision, and audience awareness also take prominent positions in my composition classes, I argue that there is more to effective writing than just generating details and revising writer-based prose into reader-based prose. Writing does not occur in a social vacuum, nor is it confined to the universalizing geometry of the rhetorical triangle. Writers invent arguments out of the values and identities they have learned through their engagement with various institutions, and they adapt their prose to the perceived needs of an audience whom they invent and invoke in social and discursive relation to themselves. In these instances, writing is situated beyond the levels of correctness and propriety. Writing is situated in *discourse* itself, in the constant flow of texts produced within the ideological confines of institutions which, according to the rules of their own discursive practices, either validate or reject the texts we write.

Thus, armed with sharpened critical and productive skills at the discursive level of finished texts and writing processes, I argue that students are better able to consume and generate documents in ways that suit the social and communal functions of language. Students who internalize social-process methods for rhetorical inquiry are not only able to expose in various texts the values and identities that are detrimental to the social health of their own communities, but they are also able to compose productive documents that either subvert those detrimental values or construct values more consistent with the needs and goals of their communities. And so, having taken a long and winding path through theory and practice, I conclude my journey with a final appeal: I urge writing teachers to incorporate social-process methodologies into their existing composition curricula, not neglecting the linguistic and rhetorical levels of composing, but rather strengthening and reinforcing them with attention to the social contexts and ideological investments that pervade both the processes and products of writing.

NOTE

1.   Although not directly called "communal democracy," the sentiments of this political formation are most notable in Lyotard's *Political*

Writings and *The Postmodern Condition,* Giroux's *Pedagogy and the Politics of Hope,* Laclau and Mouffe's *Hegemony and Socialist Strategy,* and Derrida's *The Other Heading.*

School Critical and Practical Essays: Invention

The following heuristic is designed to help you explore the formal and hidden curricula fostered in schools you attend or have attended.

Formal curriculum comprises the subjects, the contents, the facts that are overtly taught in schools. Most high schools divide their students into different "academic tracks" (e.g. vocational and college prep); these tracks have different curricula and academic requirements (e.g. courses and placement tests) serving the particular functions of each track. Most universities segment their formal curricula into "colleges" or "schools" (College of Liberal Arts, School of Engineering) and further into majors (Music Composition, Professional Writing; Electrical Engineering, Mechanical Engineering). Colleges and schools have established general guidelines that regulate what kinds of courses students should take (15 hours of Liberal Arts, 15 hours of Health Sciences), thereby also determining what general kinds of knowledge (creative, empirical) are appropriate to student members of each college or school. Majors have established specific requirements designating appropriate courses students must take in order to graduate (e.g. English 1200). Each course within the formal curriculum of a major highlights specific information and/or ways of thinking with which any X-major must be familiar.

Hidden curriculum comprises the cultural values imposed (often unconsciously) on students through specific pedagogical practices. Cultural values are statements about what is ideal: the ideal community citizen is productive, the ideal consumer of culture is responsible, the ideal subordinate respects authority. Many schools attempt to perpetuate these cultural values in their own settings. Teachers and administrators in these schools argue, for example, that education should encourage (or condition) students to become productive citizens of a community, responsible consumers of culture, and respectful subordinates. Students are taught these cultural values indirectly through pedagogical practices, such as arranging the geography of the classroom, maintaining strict classroom etiquette, structuring students' free time, and encouraging involvement in certain kinds of "healthy" or "intellectual" extracurricular activities. Schools produce certain kinds of people (ideal citizens) by teaching their students to consume culture in specific ways, by conditioning students to behave in specific ways, and by encouraging students to associate with people in specific ways.

Here are some examples of hidden curriculum at work:

Teachers and administrators use hidden curriculum strategies to encourage students to become productive citizens of a community: they require several small assignments (due every day) rather than larger assignments (due every week) to keep students in the habit of constant production; they monitor passing periods to prevent socializing, and they monitor study halls to make sure students continue to be productive even during their "free time."

Teachers and administrators use hidden curriculum strategies to encourage students to become responsible consumers of culture: they confiscate "low culture" artifacts (magazines, comic books, portable stereos, etc.) and replace them with "high culture" artifacts (canonized literature, classical music, etc.); and extracurricular activities such as band, drama, and working for the school newspaper provide for students firsthand experience with "high culture."

Teachers and administrators use hidden curriculum strategies to encourage students to become respectful subordinates: they place their own desks (usually very large ones) at the front of the room enabling constant surveillance; and teachers may speak at any time, but students must raise their hands and be recognized before speaking.

In many instances, the cultural values of the hidden curriculum are imposed on students with good intentions and positive results; however, there are also instances when these cultural values work against the personal values held by students and create conflict among members of school communities.

Following are a few prompts to help you explore the hidden curricula at the schools you attend (or have attended). Other elements of the hidden curriculum will present themselves as you explore different aspects of school.

- Describe the physical/geographical features of the entire school and some of its key spaces (the classrooms, study hall, cafeteria, gymnasium, locker bays, restrooms, assembly hall, sport fields, etc.). Explain why administrators might have arranged the physical/geographical features of your school to appear in this manner.
- Choose one or two teachers you like and one or two you do not like and describe their pedagogical practices (their interaction with students, teaching methods, disciplinary policies, grading procedures, classroom activities, etc.). Explain what it is about these pedagogical practices that makes one teacher better or worse than another.
- List the most popular extracurricular activities among students at your school; then list the least popular extracurricular activities among students at your school. Explain why some activities in your school are popular while others are not.

Through writing, we can understand and critique the hidden curricula at work in the schools we attend, and we can work to make changes in these hidden curricula for the good of our school communities.

WORKS CITED

Aronowitz, Stanley. "Postmodernism and Politics." *Social Text 6* (1987): 99-115.

Bartholomae, David. "Inventing the University." *When a Writer Can't Write: Studies in Writer's Block and Other Composing Process Problems*. Ed. Mike Rose. New York: Guilford, 1985. 134-65.

Berlin, James A. "Composition and Cultural Studies." *Composition and Resistance*. Ed. C. Mark Hurlbert and Michael Blitz. Portsmouth, NH: Boynton/Cook, 1991. 47-55.

———. "Contemporary Composition: The Major Pedagogical Theories." *College English* 44 (1982): 765-77.

———. *Rhetoric and Reality: Writing Instruction in American Colleges, 1900-1985*. Carbondale: Southern Illinois UP, 1987.

———. *Rhetorics, Poetics, and Cultures: Reforming College English Studies*. Urbana: NCTE, 1996.

Bizzell, Patricia. *Academic Discourse and Critical Consciousness*. Pittsburgh: U of Pittsburgh P, 1992.

Brent, Doug. *Reading as Rhetorical Invention: Knowledge, Persuasion, and the Teaching of Research Based Writing*. Urbana: NCTE, 1992.

Brodkey, Linda. *Writing Permitted in Designated Areas Only*. Minneapolis: U of Minnesota P, 1996.

Brown, Richard Harvey. "Social Science and Society as Discourse: Toward a Sociology for Civic Competence." *Postmodernism and Social Theory*. Ed. Steven Seidman and David G. Wagner. Cambridge, MA: Blackwell, 1992. 223-43.

Clifford, John. "The Subject in Discourse." *Contending with Words: Composition and Rhetoric in a Postmodern Age*. Ed. Patricia Harkin and John Schilb. New York: MLA, 1991. 38-51.

Crowley, Sharon. "Linguistics and Composition Instruction, 1950-1980." *Written Communication* 6 (1989): 480-505.

Derrida, Jacques. *The Other Heading: Reflections on Today's Europe*. Trans. Pascale-Anne Brault and Michael B. Naas. Bloomington: Indiana UP, 1992.

Dobrin, Sidney I. *Constructing Knowledges: The Politics of Theory-Building and Pedagogy in Composition.* New York: State U of New York P, 1997.

Donahue, Patricia, and Ellen Quandahl, eds. *Reclaiming Pedagogy: The Rhetoric of the Classroom.* Carbondale: Southern Illinois UP, 1989.

Driskill, Linda. "Understanding the Writing Context in Organizations." *Writing in the Business Professions.* Ed. Myra Kogen. Urbana: NCTE, 1989. 125-45.

Ede, Lisa, and Andrea Lunsford. "Audience Addressed/Audience Invoked: The Role of Audience in Composition Theory and Pedagogy." *College Composition and Communication* 35 (1984): 155-71.

Elbow, Peter. "Closing My Eyes as I Speak: An Argument for Ignoring Audience." *College English* 49 (1987): 50-69.

———. *Writing Without Teachers.* New York: Oxford UP, 1973.

Ellsworth, Elizabeth. "Educational Media, Ideology, and the Presentation of Knowledge through Popular Cultural Forms." *Popular Culture, Schooling, and Everyday Life.* Ed. Henry A. Giroux and Roger I. Simon. New York: Bergin and Garvey, 1989. 47-66.

Emig, Janet. *The Composing Process of 12th Graders.* Urbana: NCTE, 1971.

Faigley, Lester. *Fragments of Rationality: Postmodernity and the Subject of Composition.* Pittsburgh: U of Pittsburgh P, 1992.

Fairclough, Norman. *Critical Discourse Analysis: The Critical Study of Language.* London: Longman, 1995.

———. *Discourse and Social Change.* Cambridge: Polity, 1992.

———. *Language and Power.* London: Longman, 1989.

Fairclough, Norman, and Ruth Wodak. "Critical Discourse Analysis." *Discourse as Social Interaction.* Ed. Teun van Dijk. London: Sage, 1997. 258-84.

Farmer, Frank. "Dialogue and Critique: Bakhtin and the Cultural Studies Writing Classroom." *College Composition and Communication* 49 (1998): 186-207.

Fiske, John. *Introduction to Communication Studies.* 2nd ed. London: Routledge, 1990.

Fitts, Karen, and Alan W. France, eds. *Left Margins: Cultural Studies and Composition Pedagogy.* New York: State U of New York P, 1995.

Flower, Linda. *The Construction of Negotiated Meaning: A Social Cognitive Theory of Writing.* Carbondale: Southern Illinois UP, 1994.

Foucault, Michel. *The Order of Things: An Archeology of the Human Sciences.* New York: Vintage, 1970.

Fowler, Roger. *Language in the News: Discourse and Ideology in the Press.* London: Routledge, 1991.

Fowler, Roger, Bob Hodge, Gunther Kress, and Tony Trew. *Language and Control.* London: Routledge, 1979.

Freire, Paulo. *Education for Critical Consciousness.* New York: Continuum, 1992.

Fulkerson, Richard. "Four Philosophies of Composition." *College Composition and Communication* 30 (1979): 343-48.

George, Diana, and Diane Shoos. "Issues of Subjectivity and Resistance: Cultural Studies in the Composition Classroom." *Cultural Studies in the English Classroom.* Ed. James A. Berlin and Michael J. Vivion. Portsmouth, NH: Boynton/Cook, 1992. 200-10.

George, Diana, and John Trimbur. *Reading Culture: Contexts for Critical Reading and Writing.* 1st ed. New York: HarperCollins, 1992.

Giroux, Henry A. *Pedagogy and the Politics of Hope: Theory, Culture, and Schooling.* Boulder, CO: Westview, 1997.

Gradin, Sherrie. *Romancing Rhetorics: Social Expressivist Perspectives on the Teaching of Writing.* Portsmouth, NH: Boynton/Cook, 1995.

Grossberg, Lawrence. "Strategies of Marxist Cultural Interpretation." *Critical Perspectives on Media and Society.* Ed. Robert K. Avery and David Eason. New York: Guilford, 1991. 126-59.

Hairston, Maxine. "Diversity, Ideology, and Teaching Writing." *College Composition and Communication* 43 (1992): 179-93.

Hall, Stuart. "Encoding/Decoding." *Culture, Media, Language: Working Papers in Cultural Studies, 1972-79.* Ed. Stuart Hall, Dorothy Hobson, Andrew Lowe, and Paul Willis. London: Hutchinson, 1980. 128-38.

Halliday, M. A. K. *Explorations in the Functions of Language.* London: Edward Arnold, 1973.

———. *Grammar, Society and the Noun.* London: H. K. Lewis, 1967.

———. *Learning How to Mean: Explorations in the Development of Language.* London: Edward Arnold, 1975.

———. *Spoken and Written Language.* Oxford: Oxford UP, 1989.

———. *System and Function in Language: Selected Papers.* Ed. Gunther Kress. London: Oxford UP, 1976.

Harris, Joseph. "The Other Reader." *Composition Theory for the Postmodern Classroom.* Ed. Gary Olson and Sidney I. Dobrin. New York: State U of New York P, 1994. 225-35.

Hodge, Robert, and Gunther Kress. *Social Semiotics.* Ithaca, NY: Cornell UP, 1988.

Hurlbert, C. Mark, and Michael Blitz, eds. *Composition and Resistance.* Portsmouth, NH: Boynton/Cook, 1991.

Hurlbert, C. Mark, and Samuel Totten, eds. *Social Issues in the English Classroom.* Urbana: NCTE, 1992.

Johnson, Richard. "What Is Cultural Studies Anyway?" *Social Text* 6 (1987): 38-80.

Kent, Thomas. "Beyond System: The Rhetoric of Paralogy." *College English* 51 (1989): 492- 503.

———. "Paralogic Hermeneutics and the Possibilities of Rhetoric."*Rhetoric Review* 8 (1989): 24- 42.

Killingsworth, M. Jimmie. "Product and Process, Literacy and Orality: An Essay on Composition and Culture." *College Composition and Communication* 44 (1993): 26-39.

Kress, Gunther. *Learning to Write. 2nd ed.* London: Routledge, 1994.

———. "Representational Resources and the Production of Subjectivity: Questions for the Theoretical Development of Critical Discourse Analysis in a Multicultural Society." *Texts and Practices: Readings in Critical Discourse Analysis.* Ed. Carmen Rosa Caldas-Coulthard and Malcom Coulthard. New York: Routledge, 1996. 15-31.

———. *Writing the Future: English and the Making of a Culture of Innovation.* Urbana: NCTE, 1995.

Kress, Gunther, and Robert Hodge. *Language as Ideology.* London: Routledge, 1979.

Laclau, Ernesto, and Chantal Mouffe. *Hegemony and Socialist Strategy: Towards a Radical Democratic Politics.* London: Verso, 1985.

Lauer, Janice. "Heuristics and Composition." *College Composition and Communication* 21 (1970): 396-404.

LeFevre, Karen Burke. *Invention as a Social Act.* Carbondale: Southern Illinois UP, 1987.

Long, Russell C. "Writer-Audience Relationships: Analysis or Invention." *College Composition and Communication* 31 (1980): 221-26.

Lunsford, Andrea A., and Lisa Ede. "Representing Audience: 'Successful' Discourse and Disciplinary Critique." *College Composition and Communication* 47 (1996): 167-79.

Lyotard, Jean-François. *Political Writings.* Trans. Bill Readings and Kevin Paul Geiman. Minneapolis: U of Minnesota P, 1993.

———. *The Postmodern Condition: A Report on Knowledge.* Trans. Geoff Bennington and Brian Massumi. Minneapolis: U of Minnesota P, 1989.

Marx, Karl. "Introduction to a Critique of Political Economy." *A Contribution to the Critique of Political Economy*. Trans. S. W. Ryazanskaya. Ed. Maurice Dobb. New York: International, 1970. 188-217.

McGowan, John. *Postmodernism and Its Critics*. Ithaca: Cornell UP, 1992.

Miller, Susan. *Rescuing the Subject: A Critical Introduction to Rhetoric and the Writer*. Carbondale: Southern Illinois UP, 1989.

———. *Textual Carnivals: The Politics of Composition*. Carbondale: Southern Illinois UP, 1991.

Morley, Dave. "Texts, Readers, Subjects." *Culture, Media, Language: Working Papers in Cultural Studies, 1972-79*. Ed. Stuart Hall, Dorothy Hobson, Andrew Lowe, and Paul Willis. London: Hutchinson, 1980. 163-73.

Murray, Donald. "Teach Writing as a Process Not Product." *The Leaflet* (November 1972): 11- 14.

Norris, Christopher. *What's Wrong with Postmodernism: Critical Theory and the Ends of Philosophy*. Baltimore: Johns Hopkins, 1990.

Odell, Lee. "Beyond the Text: Relations between Writing and Social Context." *Writing in Nonacademic Settings*. Ed. Lee Odell and Dixie Goswami. New York: Guilford, 1985. 249-80.

Ong, Walter. "The Writer's Audience Is Always a Fiction." *PMLA* 90 (1975): 9-21.

Park, Douglas. "The Meanings of 'Audience.'" *College English* 44 (1982): 247-57.

Parker, Frank, and Kim Sydow Campbell. "Linguistics and Writing: A Reassessment." *College Composition and Communication* 44 (1993): 295-314.

Penrod, Diane, ed. *Miss Grundy Doesn't Teach Here Anymore: Popular Culture and the Composition Classroom*. Portsmouth, NH: Boynton/Cook, 1997.

Phelps, Louise Wetherbee. "The Dance of Discourse." *Pre/Text: The First Decade*. Ed. Victor Vitanza. Pittsburgh: U of Pittsburgh P, 1993. 31-64.

Porter, James E. *Audience and Rhetoric: An Archaeological Composition of the Discourse Community*. Englewood Cliffs, NJ: Prentice Hall, 1992.

Reither, James A. "Writing and Knowing: Toward Redefining the Writing Process." *College English* 47 (1985): 620-28.

Richardson, Kay. "Critical Linguistics and Textual Diagnosis." *Text* 7 (1987): 145-63.

Said, Edward. *Orientalism*. New York: Random House, 1978.

Sullivan, Patricia A., and Donna J. Qualley, eds. *Pedagogy in the Age of Politics: Writing and Reading (in) the Academy*. Urbana: NCTE, 1994.

Tobin, Lad. "How the Writing Process Was Born and Other Conversion Narratives." *Taking Stock: The Writing Process Movement in the 1990s.* Ed. Lad Tobin and Thomas Newkirk. Portsmouth, NH: Boynton/Cook, 1994. 1-16.

Trimbur, John. "Taking the Social Turn: Teaching Writing Post-Process." *College Composition and Communication* 45 (1994): 108-18.

Turner, Greame. *British Cultural Studies: An Introduction.* New York: Routledge, 1992.

Van Dijk, Teun A. *Elite Discourse and Racism.* Newbury Park, CA: Sage, 1993.

———. *Racism and the Press.* London: Routledge, 1991.

Yagelski, Robert. "Who's Afraid of Subjectivity? The Composing Process and Postmodernism or a Student of Donald Murray Enters the Age of Postmodernism." *Taking Stock: The Writing Process Movement in the 1990s.* Ed. Lad Tobin and Thomas Newkirk. Portsmouth, NH: Boynton/Cook, 1994. 203-18.

Young, Richard E. "Paradigms and Problems: Needed Research in Rhetorical Invention." *Research on Composition: Points of Departure.* Ed. Charles R. Cooper and Lee Odell. Urbana: NCTE, 1978. 29-47.

INDEX

ABOUT THE AUTHOR

Bruce McComiskey teaches graduate and undergraduate courses in rhetoric and writing at the University of Alabama at Birmingham, where he recently helped develop a new concentration in professional writing for English majors and a minor in writing for non-majors.

A graduate of Illinois State University and Purdue University, McComiskey moved in 1994 to Greenville, North Carolina and began teaching in the Rhetoric and Composition program at East Carolina University. While studying at Purdue, he had focused on theoretical discussions of culture and writing, but at East Carolina he began in earnest to apply cultural theory to his own view of process pedagogy and classroom practice. *Teaching Composition as a Social Process* is the result of the work he did while living and teaching in Greenville.

While McComiskey retains his devotion to social-process rhetorical inquiry, his most recent scholarship explores how Birmingham, as an urban context for teaching and writing, places unique exigencies on the inquiry processes that students engage everyday. Writing is, after all, a social process, and *place* is as much a part of "the social" as the people who live there.